Conquer Your Fear of Flying

Conquer
Your Fear
of Flying

MAEVE BYRNE CRANGLE
B.A., M.A., Ph.D.

Limerick
County Library

Newleaf

Published by
Newleaf
an imprint of
Gill & Macmillan Ltd
Hume Avenue, Park West, Dublin 12
with associated companies throughout the world
www.gillmacmillan.ie

© Maeve Byrne Crangle 2001, 2004

0 7171 3796 1

Design by Identikit
Print origination by Carrigboy Typesetting Services, Co. Cork
Printed by and bound by AIT Nørhaven A/S, Denmark

This book is typeset in Berkeley Oldstyle 10.5pt/14pt.

The paper used in this book comes from the wood pulp of managed forests. For every tree felled, at least one tree is planted, thereby renewing natural resources.

A CIP catalogue record for this book is available from the British Library.

1 3 5 4 2

Contents

Acknowledgments   viii

Preface   ix

Introduction   1

Part One

1. How Common is the Fear of Flying?   9
2. Causes of the Fear of Flying   19
3. Personal and Flight-related Fears   27
4. Flight Personnel   49
5. They Really do Fly   58
6. The Pilot's Day   67
7. Into the Future, Looking Back   74

Part Two

8. The Nature of Anxiety   85
9. Conquer Your Fear of Flying   100

10. Self-management Programme   111
11. Security and Terrorism   152
12. In-flight Health — Deep Vein Thrombosis   157
13. Nutrition and Fear of Flying   162
14. Frequently Asked Questions   175
15. Personal Flight Plan   189

Conclusion   195

Dedication

This book is dedicated to all my clients, who deserve a special tribute of praise and admiration for conquering their fear of flying.

Acknowledgments

MY DEEPEST GRATITUDE AND love to my husband John, who is a Chief Flying Instructor and has trained numerous student pilots to achieve full Commercial Airline Status. I thank him sincerely for his enlightening chapters' particularly his chapter 'Into the Future, Looking Back', which is new to this edition. I also want to express my genuine appreciation to him for all his incisive comments while writing 'Frequently Asked Questions' and in the general editing of the book.

I would also like to thank Michael Gill for his interest and encouragement in the publication of this second edition and finally, as usual, a special word of thanks to my very good friend Oggi Uomo.

Preface

IN THE COURSE OF my years of treating the problem of fear of flying I have met many people who missed wonderful opportunities as a result of being too frightened to fly. Three years have passed since the first edition of this book was published in 2001 and now many people who already read the first edition know the cause of their fear of flying, while others try to figure out where it began to go wrong for them.

The contents of the book are divided into two parts. Part One deals with the technical information as to how something as big as an aeroplane gets off the ground. It includes information to help you appreciate the function of all the flight personnel, who play a major role in ensuring the safe operation of your flight. Part Two deals with your fear and presents information to help you understand the nature of anxiety, the factors that maintain it and most important of all, a step-by-step self-management programme on how to conquer your fear of flying.

11 September 2001 has come and gone but will always remain in our memories as one of the most horrific and abhorrent acts of terrorism ever perpetrated against mankind. Its ripple effect has shocked all nations, and as a result there have been many positive changes regarding security throughout the entire airline industry.

The main reason for writing this new edition is not only to consolidate what I have already written but also to present up-to-date information, advice and reassurance on all these important issues. An additional chapter completes Part One by outlining the first century of flight. The three new chapters in Part Two describe security, in-flight health and also give answers to the questions we have been most frequently asked in the Fearless Flying Programme.

The first edition of this book has successfully helped many people break the shackles of the fear that has chained them to the ground. They are now free to fly and therefore live more fulfilling and enriching lives. The second edition can only consolidate that. Let's hope you can join them and discover new horizons!

Introduction

Pioneers of the Sky — The History of Flight

'The natural function of the wing is to soar upwards and carry that which is heavy up to the place where dwells the race of gods. More than any other thing that pertains to the body it partakes of the divine.'

Plato, Phaedres

'Imagination is more powerful than knowledge.'

Einstein

MAN'S DREAM OF BEING able to fly was first conceived in his imagination and from time immemorial mankind has had a fascination with flight. Thanks to the ingenuity, Trojan work and determination of the early pioneers of flight, gigantic strides have been made in the field of aviation down through the years. The twentieth century saw unimaginable progress and development in aviation, especially with the invention of jet flight. Access to almost any country in the world is now possible. Magellan and his fleet took three years to circumnavigate the world. Nowadays air travellers can complete the same journey in less than two days. A transatlantic flight from Ireland takes approximately seven hours. A few years ago an Aer Lingus jet flew eastbound across the Atlantic in four and a half hours. This is inconceivable when you consider that it took Christopher Columbus 71 days to cross the same ocean. Air transport has undoubtedly revolutionised civilisation in ways that the early trail-blazers could not have possibly envisaged. Air travel, which is taken for granted today, owes its origins to man's attempt to unravel the secrets of flight by observing the movements of birds through the air. From earliest times he had a vision of creatures other than birds being able to fly. Stories from the mythology of early civilisations frequently portrayed deities, monsters, animals and men as having wings, thereby being endowed with the gift of flight. As far back as 3,000 B.C. Babylonian artists illustrated the story of Etana the flying shepherd, while the Egyptians had a winged god and the Assyrians a winged bull. One of the earliest stories of flight tells of Daedalus and his son Icarus who flew on feathered wings.

Most people associate the Wright brothers with the advent of flight; however, the early pioneers of flight go back much further. In fact it was in the thirteenth century that one of the earliest investigators of flight, Friar Roger Bacon, made proposals for a mechanical bird. Three hundred years later the Jesuit Francesco de Lana designed a brilliant but totally unworkable airship. Time moved on and in 1709 the Portuguese Father Gusmao is credited with having actually flown a model glider and also a model hot-air balloon.

The great Leonardo da Vinci was the first man to emphasise scientific facts on dreams of flight. 'A bird', he said, 'is an instrument working according to mathematical laws, which instrument is within the capacity of man to reproduce in all its movements.' Da Vinci designed various flying machines which depended upon considerable horsepower or muscle power for their successful operation. The concept of engine power had not been developed in that era; consequently it was impossible for da Vinci to adequately test his designs, given the amount of power available. Many centuries later the IBM company recreated some of Leonardo's flying models, attached engines to them and proved that they do work.

Throughout the nineteenth century considerable aeronautical progress was forged by experiments with 'lighter-than-air' flight and 'heavier-than-air' machines. A lighter-than-air craft is one that rises by means of an agent, such as hot air or gas, whose density is lighter than the atmosphere around it. Experiments led from balloons to airships and formed an exciting phase in flying history.

The balloon era was initiated in 1783 when the Montgolfier brothers built a small hot-air balloon and successfully flew it. The balloon was a spherical-shaped linen and paper bag, open at one end and mounted above a fire which heated the air within and caused the device to rise to a height of 6,000 feet. In the same year the first air travellers were a cock, a duck and a sheep, and they successfully ascended in a Montgolfier balloon from Versailles, outside Paris.

In that same year the first human passenger flight in history took place when Frenchman Pilatre de Rozier and a companion took off in a hot-air balloon from a garden in the Bois de Boulogne, outside Paris. They were cheered on by thousands of enthusiastic spectators as the balloon ascended to a height of approximately 300 feet and drifted five and a half miles across Paris in a timespan of 25 minutes.

Shortly after this exciting event, a second passenger flight was made by Professor Jacques Charles and a friend. Charles had made important progress by inventing the hydrogen balloon in which they ascended, stayed aloft longer and flew further, a distance of 27 miles from Paris to the village of Nesle. Two years later, in 1785, more aeronautical progress was made when Jean Blanchard and Dr John Jeffries crossed the English Channel in a gas-filled balloon. In Ireland there was great interest in this new venture of flight. This was the year that saw the first balloon ascent in Ireland, made by Wicklow man Richard Crosbie, who ascended from Ranelagh Gardens in Dublin and drifted as far as the North Strand. Several years later, in 1817, the Irish Sea was crossed by William Sadler, who ascended from Portobello Barracks in Dublin and safely landed in the Isle of Anglesey six hours later. In 1844 the American public's imagination was whetted by a fictitious account of a balloon crossing of the Atlantic. This creative report was written by Edgar Allan Poe, published on the front page of the *New York Sun* as fact and read avidly by its readers.

The nineteenth century marked a very important phase in aviation history when experiments conducted with balloons progressed to airships. In 1852 a steerable balloon — known as a dirigible — was developed by French engineer Henri Giffard. Instead of hot air or hydrogen gas, this craft was flown by Giffard, who continuously stoked its underslung steam engine to maintain its momentum. The turn of the twentieth century saw the invention of the first practical rigid dirigible, which was built by Count von Zeppelin, using an aluminium framework approximately 400 feet in length. He flew the giant aircraft from Lake Constance in Germany, ascending to a height of 1,300 feet at a speed of 8 miles per hour. Zeppelin's remained the best of such large-scale aircraft until the 1930s, when production ceased following a series of tragic disasters.

In pursuit of making the vision of flight a reality, progress was achieved through a variety of inventions throughout the world. One of the most prominent pioneer inventors of these times was Sir George Cayley, who is responsible for laying the foundation of modern aerodynamics. Cayley constructed very effective model gliders. One day in 1853 he sent his coachman aloft in a full-sized machine across a valley in Brompton, now marked as the first gliding flight in history. In England and France steam-powered aeroplanes were designed in the late 1800s which were completely successful. Between 1896 and 1901 Samuel Langley, an American scientist, flew some wonderful model tandem-wing aircraft. The development of aviation was also being pursued in Australia, when in 1893 the inventor Lawrence Hargrave designed the box-kite. Hargrave is attributed with other important work that proved vital in the development of some of Europe's early aircraft.

It was in the latter part of the nineteenth century that a German designer successfully flew a steadily improving variety of air-worthy gliders, paving the way for man to conquer the air and fly. However, one of the major problems for aircraft designers still remained — the question of how to devise a light-weight power unit and steering device. The solution to the first part of this problem was eventually resolved by Gottlieb Daimler when he developed the four-cycle internal combustion engine, originally invented in 1876.

The first practical, powered aeroplane was designed not by aircraft designers or engineers or indeed scientists, but by two bicycle mechanics, Wilbur and Orville Wright, who lived in Dayton, Ohio. The Wright brothers made a meticulous and comprehensive study of all the available data. In 1900–02 they built three gliders and concentrated on becoming completely proficient at flying and control. Not until they were competent at flight control, in particular banked turns, did they endeavour to construct a powered machine. It is absolutely true to say that the Wright brothers were the first to build a practical, powered aeroplane. In 1903 they built a biplane powered by a 12 horsepower internal combustion engine with cambered wings spanning 40 feet and with two propellers.

History records 17 December 1903 as the dawn of aviation. On that great day, Orville took off in the little biplane from Kill Devil Hills, near Kitty Hawk, North Carolina. He flew a ground distance of 120 feet in 12 seconds. Later that morning Wilbur flew an air distance of half a mile in 59 seconds. At last the age-old question had been answered. It was now possible to steer the aircraft and man's vision of flight had become a reality. An exhilarating new era opened and from that day forward the world has never been the same.

PART ONE

CHAPTER ONE

How Common is the Fear of Flying?

DOWN THROUGH THE CENTURIES, countless people have associated an aura of excitement, awe and romance with air travel. In the twenty-first millennium, air transport is seen as a means to an end rather than an end in itself. Man's knowledge of the world has expanded and international aviation has contributed much more than a transport service for people and consumer goods. Air travel has become increasingly important from a broad range of perspectives, which include personal, business, humanitarian and political among others.

The inability to travel by air is perceived by numerous aerophobics and fearful fliers as a major handicap. As a result of this problem, many restrictions are imposed on the quality of their lives in terms of their ability to pursue business development, career promotions and personal relationships. Recreational pursuits such as holidays, cultural, scientific and other educational interests have also been seriously affected by sufferers of this problem.

Although aviation specialists estimate that increasing numbers of people are flying further afield more frequently than at any other time in our civilisation, the fear of flying is a very common problem which has long been a subject of popular and professional interest. It is a topic of fascination and is often a subject of discussion on television, radio shows and magazine articles.

Fear of Flying is Not a Modern Affliction

Fear of flying is not as modern a phenomenon as many believe. Anxiety associated with flying has been reported since man first flew. Early studies of the problem focused on military air crews. Psychological reactions to flying were initially studied during World War One when high psychiatric casualty rates were recorded among military air crews. After approximately 10 hours of flight training, these men became fighter pilots and immediately commenced combat in the air. In 1919 Dr H. E. Anderson investigated the problem among some military pilots and diagnosed their symptoms as a fear of flying. His observations and recommendations initiated much of what has been written since. According to Anderson' many experienced 'unhappiness in the air and morbid thoughts' which required prompt psychological attention. He coined the term 'aeroneurosis' for the variety of symptoms resulting in a reluctance to fly. Other doctors at that time included the following among the symptoms related to a fear of flying:

- mental and physical exhaustion
- conduct disorders
- traumatic physical experiences.

As with many other areas of science, technology and human relations, World War Two was the watershed for understanding the psychological disorder of the fear of flying. During and after World War Two more in-depth studies on the nature of flight-related anxiety among military air crews appeared. Descriptions of men suffering psychic trauma during and after combat were similar but more intense than those noted in World War One. Sleeplessness, nervousness, agitation, physical complaints, nightmares and phobic responses to planes were noted. Treatment at that time consisted of counselling, convalescent leave and rest.

With the development and increasing importance of commercial aviation, the fear of flying as experienced by the airline passenger began to receive more attention. As larger air transport carriers emerged, air travel became accessible to more than an elitist few. Increasing numbers of airlines offered competitive air fares, bonus points for frequent air travellers and package deals to attractive destinations. Travelling by air became an affordable option available for the majority. However, as the number of passengers travelling by air increased each year, more and more people began to find air travel a daunting and traumatic experience.

It was in the late 1960s and early 1970s that air travel anxiety among civilian passengers was first studied. Psychologists and psychiatrists devised successful treatment methods to help sufferers overcome the problem. The good news resulting from these studies and treatments showed that irrespective of the length of time one had this problem or the severity of the condition, the fear of flying was definitely a reversible condition for the majority of sufferers. In response to cries for help from the public, many major international airlines offer courses to enable anxious passengers to cope with their fear and travel more comfortably.

Prevalence of Fear of Flying

The fear of flying is a problem that can develop in anyone, irrespective of age, socio-economic status, career background or indeed air travel experience. Many regular passengers who fly frequently on short flights or long-haul trips are quite startled when they realise they are developing this fear. It is a problem that can affect young and old. The youngest client I worked with was seven years old, and the oldest client to date was a delightful 75-year-old lady who hadn't flown for 40 years and has since travelled extensively throughout Europe.

Fearful fliers come from all walks of life and backgrounds. They can be found among home-makers, school teachers, solicitors, doctors, church ministers, business executives, bankers, politicians, artists, journalists and entertainers. It will come as no surprise that many people in the travel industry have suffered a problem with flying. On a worldwide basis, more women than men admit to being fearful of flying, but researchers generally believe that women are more willing to come forward for help. Certainly in Ireland there seem to be marginally more women than men who suffer from the problem. Over the last decade the average age of those seeking help was in the mid-40s to 50s bracket, but this is now changing as increasing numbers of younger businessmen and women in their late 20s and early 30s seek help for what they describe as a crippling fear. Many are apprehensive that if they don't overcome their fear of air travel, it will inevitably affect their career prospects.

According to aviation specialists who treat this problem, over 500 million people worldwide have a severe fear of flying. The Boeing Aircraft Corporation carried out a study on the subject 20 years ago and found that 25 million Americans were afraid to fly. More recent estimates suggest that this figure has now risen to over 30 million. The prevalence of this problem has been studied in other countries such as Australia, which showed that 20 per cent of the population are afraid to fly. Fifty per cent of the Dutch population have never flown and 28 per cent confess to being too frightened to fly. It is reckoned that in the United Kingdom one in every 15 adults experiences intense fear when flying, while the results of a study of 1,000 people in Iceland showed that 18 per cent were afraid of flying. The problem was also examined in the Scandinavian countries of Norway and Sweden, which found that of 1,000 Norwegians studied, 22 per cent reported acute anxiety when flying and 5 per cent refuse to fly. In Sweden a similar study showed that 36 per cent admitted to feeling very apprehensive when flying and 8 per cent admitted to a severe fear at the prospect of boarding an aeroplane.

In addition to having a fear of air travel, many fear admitting they have such a problem, which increases an already stress-loaded situation. Some believe it is socially unacceptable to admit to a fear of flying; still more find it embarrassing and say they feel ashamed of their fear; many see the problem as a sign of personal weakness. Their usual method of masking it is to say they just don't like it, or make excuses: 'It's a better idea if we take the ferry. We can take the car and see more of the countryside.'

Lengths to which People Go to Avoid Flying

Business executives who are compelled to fly on company business are among those most seriously affected. One passenger described how he suffered so much before flying to important business meetings that by the time he arrived he could hardly function coherently. He was totally drained and couldn't get the horror of making the return flight out of his mind for the duration of the meeting. Many businesspeople describe how they spent days, in some cases weeks, depending on the destination, travelling overland to attend business meetings or conferences rather than take a flight that would transport them to their destination in a matter of hours. An executive businessman related how he spent four days travelling to Paris and four days on the return journey, while his colleagues flew to the meeting in an hour and a half. Numerous people have either refused career promotions or resigned from jobs that would entail frequent air travel. Many now have a stipulation written into their contract that under no circumstances will they be obliged to fly.

There are many accounts of victims booking holidays and losing their deposits when they decided not to travel. Others have actually deserted family and friends just as they were about to board the aeroplane or just before the aircraft door closed. One Christmas Eve some years ago a young woman travelling to Switzerland with her family for the holiday jumped up and ran off the aircraft before the door closed. Her family flew on to Switzerland while she spent Christmas alone in a London hotel. One of the most extreme cases concerns a young man who spent two years flying to various destinations across Europe on a working holiday. His ambition was to travel to the Far East, which he successfully achieved. Unfortunately, when he was there he developed a severe fear of flying and spent months travelling overland on his return journey home. A fear of flying can strike any time, but help is now available.

Among fearful fliers it is interesting to note that slightly over 50 per cent of them believe that flying is not dangerous. Only a very small percentage worry about their nearest and dearest travelling by air; the majority have no such problem. They only worry about themselves flying and that the aeroplane they are travelling on will not develop any serious problems. Many who are fearful will continue to travel uncomfortably by air, but the course of action for many others who are terrified is to avoid the situation. Undoubtedly avoidance gives relief from the fear, but unfortunately avoidance only strengthens the fear.

An Irrational Fear

In general, aerophobics agree that their fear is totally irrational, illogical and unreasonable. An example of this irrationality was given by one client who plucked up his courage to fly from Dublin to Tenerife with his family. For the entire duration of the four-hour flight he was terrified, while the others were quite comfortable and enjoyed the flight. On arrival at their destination, they took a taxi to their hotel. Despite the fact that the driver seemed to be under the influence of alcohol and drove dangerously at high speed, this man relaxed completely, delighted that he wasn't flying, while the others were quite realistically terrified they were going to have a serious accident at any moment. He said that he didn't care if the driver did somersaults with the car as long as he was back on the ground.

Another example of the irrationality of this problem relates to a journalist who was sent by his editor to report on events unfolding in a country of tremendous political unrest. When asked by concerned family and friends if he was fearful of taking on this assignment, he admitted that he was far more fearful of flying overseas than actually working in a dangerous war-torn country.

Some have admitted they were unable to enjoy the excitement of their wedding preparations because they were so worried about their honeymoon flight. They went through the trauma of the flight as they did not want to disappoint their new spouse by cancelling the trip. On the other hand, it is not unknown for honeymoon trips to have been cancelled to locations such as Hawaii, Bali, Australia and, even closer to home, the romantic city of Paris due to a fear of air travel. Family members have missed special family celebrations such as weddings in beautiful countries like the Seychelles and Barbados due to the same problem.

For some, the duration of the flight is more important than the destination. One person said, 'It doesn't matter where I'm going, it's the length of the flight.' Another said, 'When my husband brings home the travel brochures for our annual holiday, I immediately become despondent and I browse through them looking for destinations that involve the least amount of flying time.' Yet another stated, 'I don't care where we go. My husband accuses me of being totally unenthusiastic and we inevitably end up having a dramatic row and I am in bad humour for days.'

A trip that millions could only dream about was refused by Grainne following her graduation from university when her favourite Australian aunt offered her a present of a round-the-world trip with all expenses paid. Her aunt wrote to her saying that she couldn't understand how a young woman could refuse such a wonderful opportunity, but Grainne insisted that she didn't mind not going because of her fear of flying. She really didn't want the gift and felt that she wasn't missing out on anything. In fact it was a relief for her not to have to put herself through such a horrendous ordeal.

'No one really understands how I feel' is a remark heard frequently. 'When we are out with friends my problem becomes a topic of conversation, with one friend trying to outdo the other with stories of outrageous incidents on flights. They don't seem to realise how this is affecting me.' Other sufferers resent how 'everyone seems to be an authority on my fear of flying. Even though flying doesn't bother them, I'm forever being advised to pull myself together or take a few brandies or tranquillisers or, better still, a sleeping pill, but this advice doesn't work.'

It is clear from the above examples that the experience is seen as a major ordeal and can have serious repercussions on the lifestyle of the individual.

Personality Traits of the Fearful Flier

People frequently ask, 'My parents were terrified of flying. Have I inherited their fear?' or 'I've always been afraid of flying ever since I was a child. I've no recollection of ever hearing anything bad about flying, but the fear has been there for as long as I can remember. Is it possible I'm born with this fear?' Others state, 'I just don't understand why I'm afraid of flying. I have never had a bad experience on a flight, everyone in our family flies quite happily except me and I feel so stupid and inadequate. Is this a flaw in my personality?' Aerophobics, along with those who are prone to anxiety disorders and phobias, tend to share certain personality traits, including positive traits such as intelligence and creativity. Other qualities that tend to intensify anxiety and interfere with self-esteem and confidence include perfectionism, the need to have things under control and an overly cautious attitude in general. Others describe themselves as being of an easy-going disposition while also admitting to being of a nervous disposition or a worrier, which is a complete contradiction.

Hereditary Components of Fear

Based on evidence to date, it appears that you do not inherit irrational fears such as claustrophobia, agoraphobia or panic attacks from your parents. What is inherited seems to be a per-sonality type that makes you more inclined to be overly anxious. However, it is important to be aware of the fact that many who have a hereditary tendency to develop one of these problems do not. The generally accepted conclusion is that most human behaviour develops as a result of a combination of parental/childhood experiences, environmental and family influences.

Childhood and Family Influences

Childhood experiences and family influences can also be relevant factors, in certain cases, to predisposing many individuals to anxiety disorders. Well-meaning parents, who are possibly more nervous than the average and who are loving and caring in every possible way towards their children, frequently admonish them to be careful when riding their bicycles or climbing trees or not to sit at the back of the bus for fear of an accident. As a result of such warnings from overprotective parents, what is communicated to the child is to be ultra careful and not to trust anybody. Children may therefore grow up with a tendency to be over-cautious in situations and places where danger is unlikely to exist.

The Role of Perfectionism

It has already been said that perfectionism can also contribute to anxiety disorders. Perfectionists set unrealistically high standards for themselves and others. They are inclined to be over-anxious about their achievements and any minor defects in themselves. They may achieve levels of performance that others consider normal or even above normal, but if their personal expectations fall short, they see themselves as failures and become critical and disappointed. Perfectionism is frequently a cause of insecurity and low self-esteem. As a result of their lack of confidence, perfectionists invariably avoid entering situations where there is a possibility of looking foolish in front of others. Such people are highly critical of their inability to fly with ease and confidence and see their fear of flying as a sign of weakness or a defect in their personality.

Those who are excessively cautious dislike not having certain situations under their control and lack confidence in themselves when others take over. This is significant when flying in an aeroplane.

CHAPTER TWO

Causes of the Fear of Flying

APART FROM FAMILY INFLUENCES and personality characteristics, there are other important factors which may cause a fear of flying and it is commonly thought that this fear can be associated with a bad experience which actually happened when flying. Certainly there are many who link their fear with turbulence or a flight that had a technical problem which for obvious reasons had to be rectified before travelling onwards to their destination. However, many others admit they have never encountered either turbulence or a technical problem, in fact all their flights were completely smooth and calm and they have no idea how or why the fear developed. Many air travellers are now more concerned about airport security and the possibility of future acts of terrorism. There are many diverse causes for this problem. Some can pinpoint the exact cause, while others cannot. This is quite common and not unusual.

Terms of Reference
Many fearful fliers say that not having any terms of reference when travelling by air, especially at night, is quite daunting and

makes them feel particularly vulnerable. Whether flying in daytime or at night really doesn't matter. No forward view as to where they are going and only a lateral view through the cabin window sends confusing signals to the brain. Naturally at night, with a darkened cabin window, this makes the reference points even harder to identify.

Outcome of a Trip

Others believe that when travelling to an important business meeting, which naturally causes genuine concern, they feel that the flight coupled with their apprehension makes for an absolutely nerve-wrecking flight.

Family Influences

Travel anxiety often starts in childhood when children take their cues of behaviour from parents or adults they are close to. Adults can unintentionally transmit their fears to children. If children are aware that their parents or favourite aunts or uncles are nervous about flying, many respond similarly, believing it is appropriate to be nervous when flying.

Maternal Instinct

It is also a universal fact that more women than men are fearful of flying. Many women say they quite enjoyed flying until they had children. Many express their fears: 'What will happen to my children if something happens to me when taking a flight?' or 'I'd hate to miss seeing my children grow up.' Many couples find that they become more responsible when they have a family, particularly women, whose protective, maternal instinct comes to the fore at the prospect of doing something they perceive as life threatening.

Lack of Knowledge

Lack of knowledge with regard to normal engine noise and aircraft movements and sensations contributes enormously towards fear. Information on the technical aspects of aviation and flight personnel is presented in Chapters 4 and 5, which will help you understand and clarify distorted beliefs you may have about the unknown elements of the ongoing flight situation.

Media

The media play a part in sowing the seeds of fear regarding air travel. They are more inclined to publish reports and articles about crowded skies, overworked pilots and air traffic controllers and delays at airports than about the positive aspects of aviation. If a major disaster occurs, the media report the tragedy with graphic description and speculation about what went wrong. Such an event is almost guaranteed prominent cover and can be a major news item for days. For example, if a flight overshoots an airport runway or the pilot does what is known as a 'go around procedure', this inevitably makes a news item in the daily papers, even though the pilots are thoroughly trained to handle such a manoeuvre. If a two-seater aircraft makes a safe emergency landing in the Amazon jungle, this also is likely to make a news feature, whereas if a coach full of children or senior citizens crashes into a river with loss of life, it does not have the same impact.

Many fliers confess that not only do they compulsively watch television programmes and read all the reports about any air disaster that occurs, but they also surf the net seeking such information. They latch on to these reports, which serve no purpose other than to add more fuel to their fear and support their conviction that they should not fly. Aviation experts are more precise in their analysis of aviation accidents. Their reports take months of painstaking research before their results and conclusions regarding the cause of an accident are published. If the disaster has been aircraft related, they always make recommendations for improvements or adjustments to ensure that such an accident will never happen again. Perhaps some solace can be taken from the words of Mark Twain: 'A person only moves forward from a failure, never from a success.'

Major Life Events

Experts maintain that phobias, panic attacks and feelings of apprehension can be attributed to times of increased stress or major upheavals in our lives. Many claim their fear of flying developed following a crisis point in their lives or after they had experienced a severe shock.

Stressful Life Changes

While some people are aware that their fear of flying developed following a severe shock or crisis point in their lives, others who flew for years without a problem admit to being totally mystified as to how their fear developed. On investigation it frequently transpires that they had experienced ongoing stressful situations or major life changes over a period of time prior to the onset of their fear of flying.

Stress is an unavoidable fact of life which affects everybody. Stress results when there is a mismatch between an individual's perception of a situation and their ability to cope with the demands of the situation. Individuals are unique and what may be a cause of stress for one may be viewed with indifference or excitement by another.

A certain level of stress arousal is good and is essential to enable us to focus the mind and energy to achieve success and meet certain goals. There are many major life changes or events which are intrinsically stressful, such as the death of a loved one, serious illness, divorce, financial difficulties or unresolved emotional traumas. When stress becomes excessive and persists over many months or years, it tends to accumulate. If our reaction is inappropriate, the body's immune system becomes undermined and makes the individual susceptible to mental, physical or psychological problems. As a result of this ongoing stress arousal, the most vulnerable point of the body's system will be affected, which may result in high blood pressure, stomach problems, anxiety disorders, panic attacks or phobias. While other factors may cause these problems, experts believe that cumulative stress can play a significant part.

The following 'Life Events Survey', which was compiled by Dr Thomas Holmes and Richard Rahe in 1981, can test the amount of stress a person can cope with in a two-year cycle. If you want to assess your personal level of cumulative stress, fill out the questionnaire and score it as directed.

Life Events Survey

	Average stress score
Death of spouse	100
Divorce	73
Marital separation	65
Jail term	63
Death of close family member	63
Personal injury or illness	53
Marriage	50
Being fired from work	47
Marital problems	45
Retirement	45
Change in health of family member	44
Pregnancy	40
Sexual difficulties	39

→

Life Events Survey *(cont'd)*

	Average stress score
Gain of a new family member	39
Business readjustment	39
Change in finances	38
Death of close friend	37
Change to different line of work	36
Change in number of arguments with spouse	35
Mortgage/loan for major purchase, e.g. a home	31
Foreclosure of mortgage or loan	30
Change in responsibilities at work	29
Son or daughter leaving home	29
Trouble with in-laws	29
Outstanding personal achievement	28
Spouse begins or stops work	26
Beginning or finishing school	26
Change in living conditions	25
Revision of personal habits	24
Trouble with boss	23
Change in work hours or conditions	20
Change in residence	20
Change in school	20
Change in recreation	19
Change in church activities	19
Change in social activities	18
Loan for lesser purchase, e.g. car or TV	17
Change in sleeping habits	16
Change in number of family get-togethers	15
Change in eating habits	15

→

Life Events Survey (*cont'd*)

	Average stress score
Vacation	13
Christmas	12
Minor violations of the law	11

Decide which life events have occurred in your life over the past two years and add up your total stress score. For example:

1. If you got married	50
2. Changed to a different line of work	36
3. Changed residence	20
4. Took a vacation	13
Your total stress score would be	119

If your total stress score is under 150, you are not likely to be suffering from stress. If it is between 150 and 300, you may be suffering from chronic stress, depending on how you perceived and coped with the particular life events that occurred. If your score is over 300, it is likely you are experiencing some detrimental effects of cumulative stress. Please note that the stress scores on the above survey are averaged over many people. It must be clearly understood that this questionnaire is only a survey and must not be taken as a prognosis.

Many rebuke themselves because they have a problem with flying; however, self-criticism is a useless exercise in this situation and merely adds to their distress. The important thing to realise is that it is not necessary to know the cause in order to overcome the problem. Many wait until their fear is at an intolerable level before seeking help.

The first step towards overcoming the fear lies in admitting to yourself that you have a problem and the second step is to look for help. The longer you avoid doing so, the stronger and deeper the problem becomes. Irrespective of the duration of the problem, its severity or the age of the individual, it has been repeatedly shown that the fear of flying is definitely a reversible problem and the majority of sufferers respond successfully to intervention. Those who for one reason or another had stopped flying for varying periods of time and who received treatment have conquered their fear and are now happily jetting all over the world.

CHAPTER THREE

Personal and Flight-related Fears

TRAVELLING BY AIR INVOLVES exposure to many sounds, sensations and movements outside the range of those normally experienced on the ground. Flying involves travelling at approximately 600 miles per hour at a great height with no sensation of speed, enclosed in a restricted environment. Passengers are also exposed to unexpected vertical and horizontal movements, especially when flying through turbulent conditions. It would not be unusual for those who are frightened of air travel to be frightened of other situations. Generally speaking, the fear of flying consists of a cluster of fears which are essentially part of the flight situation. For some the fears involved may be experienced individually, while others may have a combination of flight-related fears, such as the fear of enclosed spaces and the fear of heights. All these fears surface when taking a flight. Many nervous travellers acknowledge that the fear starts to build up after they have made a commitment to take a flight. The closer to their departure date, the worse the fear becomes.

The fear of flying is related to a package of fears which can be divided into two categories. The first consists of personal fears and the second involves flight-related fears. Many fliers state that they trust the pilot and the technology implicitly; it is themselves they do not trust. Their fears relate to the following areas.

Personal Fears

A Situation Where You Have No Control

One of the most commonly expressed fears relates to the issue of control. Many anxious air travellers are terrified of being in a situation in which they have absolutely no control whatsoever. They fear relinquishing control of their destiny to an unknown and unseen individual. As they are normally in positions of responsibility and control, they readily admit that they prefer to be in the driver's seat in almost every situation. In his work with aerophobics, the American psychologist M. Aronson described the aerophobic as follows:

> 'The ambitious, hard-driving, successful person who seeks help for his flying phobia is especially likely to become anxious if he does not have things under control. He abhors the passivity inherent in the role of an airline passenger. He becomes fearful and angry during a flight because it requires that he be immobilised, fly on someone's schedule and depend totally on strangers. Even slight increases in his anxiety level threaten his image of himself as a person who is always in charge.'

People who have a need for control prefer to have everything in life predetermined and under their command. In many instances individuals who are unsure of themselves, especially in situations or circumstances where they feel intimidated, are inclined to take self-protective action. When people who do not trust themselves or others, find themselves in situations which they perceive as threatening, they end up perpetually protecting themselves irrationally. They hate being in situations where they have no control and playing the role of a passive airline passenger goes against the grain of their personality. For such people, when contemplating the prospect of taking a flight, the emotional force of fear is stronger than their intellectual reasoning and the flight is perceived as a life or death situation. The ordeal of taking a flight in this frame of mind conflicts with their natural instinct for survival.

The issue of control can also be linked to a lack of trust in the pilot's ability and the aeroplane's technology. But flying is not the only situation whereby you surrender control to another individual. When you hail a taxi you must trust that the driver will take you to your destination safely. If you are ill and visit your doctor you must trust his or her diagnosis of your problem. When you give a prescription to the pharmacist, equally you must trust him or her to dispense the medicine correctly. If you need to undergo surgery you must trust the anaesthetist and the surgeon. You must accept the fact that you are often in a situation in which others have control. What you should aim to achieve is control of your fear in the situation and trust the experts in charge.

Fear of Enclosed Spaces

The fear of enclosed spaces is called claustrophobia, which can occur as an isolated phobia. Claustrophobics are frightened of being shut in enclosed spaces, such as small rooms, locked rooms, tunnels, lifts, subway trains and crowded areas. Individuals who fear one of these situations tend to fear them all.

Understandably, claustrophobics find travelling in an aeroplane an extremely daunting and frightening experience. When considering the cabin environment of an aeroplane, with its narrow aisles and confined seating space, it is understandable that claustrophobics perceive themselves as trapped. They are in a situation in which they are unable to stop the vehicle moving or to open a door or window. They have no avenue of escape from the source of their anxiety until the flight ends. Many claustrophobics worry there is insufficient air available to them in enclosed spaces, which in turn gives rise to a fear of difficulties in breathing and the fear of suffocation. It is possible that being confined in the enclosed space of an aircraft would accentuate these fears. With the exception of a small adjustable air vent that is located in a panel above each passenger's seat, there is no other visible source of air inflow in the cabin. Be assured that there is a complete change of air throughout the cabin every few minutes, which is generated by the engines.

Fear of Heights

A mild fear of heights is quite common in many people, but a severe, incapacitating phobia of heights, which is called acrophobia, is rare. Whether or not people are frightened of a particular height largely depends upon the details of their surroundings. Fear of heights has been reported by a considerable number of flight phobics in various studies around the world. Linked to the fear of heights is the fear of falling, if there is no support within a few feet, and the fear of being drawn over the edge, as if pulled by a magnetic force. Travelling at an altitude of 32,000 feet in a confined space, with no opportunity to end the experience until a predetermined destination is reached, can be terrifying. If a person has a fear of heights and a fear of the aircraft crashing, it is a powerful enough reason for them to be afraid of flying.

Fear of Having a Panic Attack

There are many who insist they have no fear of flying, crashing or turbulence. What they fear above all else is the possibility of having a panic attack during the flight. Many adults experience panic attacks in normal everyday circumstances, such as driving, shopping in supermarkets, going into crowded places, restaurants and attending public performances. When someone experiences a panic attack, their instinctive response is to run away from the situation. They usually associate that specific environment with their panic attack and then proceed to avoid that place or similar places. It is important to understand that panic attacks are not caused by the environment. They result from a combination of biological and psychological reactions that over-stress the body. The symptoms of a panic attack can include some of the following:

- shortness of breath
- rapid heart rate or palpitations
- pains or discomfort in the chest
- feeling smothered
- feeling as though you are choking
- feeling faint or dizzy
- feelings of unreality
- wanting to go to the toilet
- tingling in the extremities or numbness
- hot and cold flushes
- trembling muscles or shaking
- feeling nauseous.

One former fearful flier described her fear of panicking and losing all self-control as follows: 'I'm terrified of losing control. I fear I'm going to either implode or explode. I'm scared I will not be able to contain my fear and that I'll get hysterical, tear off my clothes and run up and down the cabin screaming.'

Specific thoughts go hand in hand with comments such as 'I can't breathe. I'm scared I'm going to die.' 'I feel faint, I'm afraid I'm losing control.' 'I've pains in my chest. I'm terrified I'm going to have a heart attack.' 'Everything seems so unreal. I fear I'm losing my mind.' 'I can't stop trembling. I'm having a stroke.'

These thoughts and feelings are usually accompanied by a dreadful sense of foreboding of impending doom or overwhelming feelings of terror. Those who experience these feelings prefer to avoid situations that they perceive, incorrectly, to be the cause of such feelings of fear. Fear of fear, or phobophobia, then develops and rather than run the risk of experiencing these distressing symptoms on board an aeroplane, where escape from the situation is impossible, they avoid flying.

No research to date can definitely specify the origin of panic attacks. Researchers believe that either psychological or biological reasons are the root cause why some people have panic attacks and others do not. Some researchers attribute panic attacks to conditions such as hypoglycaemia, hyperthyroidism, anaemia or hypersensitivity to caffeine. Other theories about their physical cause range from hormonal and chemical imbalances to a condition known as mitral valve prolapse (MVP), a bulging of a cardiac valve, which according to current research is regarded as harmless. MVP is a condition that occurs mostly in women and is a cause of irregular heartbeat, heart palpitations, shortness of breath, dizziness and fatigue. If you suffer from this condition it is advisable to consult your family doctor, who in all probability will reassure you that even though you do experience rapid heartbeat or palpitations when flying, the symptoms are not dangerous.

Undoubtedly the feelings and thoughts associated with panic attacks are terrifying for many sufferers, but the good news is that there is no evidence that anyone has had a heart attack, gone insane or died during a panic attack. It is important to realise that while what you are experiencing is extremely unpleasant and disturbing, no harm will come to you. The symptoms of fear are not life threatening or dangerous.

One of the major symptoms of panic attacks is an overwhelming feeling of terror, physical fear and threat. Similar symptoms are produced by the fight or flight response when the physical sensations of anxiety are triggered by the brain interpreting a given situation as dangerous or threatening. A message is sent from the brain to the adrenal glands, which in turn release the chemical adrenaline into the bloodstream, which prepares the body to cope with the perceived dangerous situation. The fight or flight response will be dealt with comprehensively in a later section.

Comfort Zone

Most people fear unfamiliar events more than those they are accustomed to on a daily basis. In addition to the personal anxieties already covered, separation anxiety is another issue many fearful fliers must contend with. When you take a flight you experience separation not only from the ground, but also from the security of your normal everyday environment. While many love the excitement and adventure of exploring beautiful cities and tasting different food, many others who travel for a holiday or for social reasons frequently say that they dislike being in a foreign country where they cannot speak the language. They don't like foreign food or the climate and find it a bit of a chore trying to orientate themselves and find their way around a foreign city. Executive business people travelling on behalf of their companies sometimes state that in addition to their fear of flying and their apprehension when negotiating business contracts, they also dislike being away from home and regard themselves as 'home birds'. They find they are inclined to worry about their families and miss the affection and security of their comfort zone. Many state that flying to exotic destinations and staying in five-star hotels soon loses its glamour when they are genuinely home-sick. Others admit that they cannot enjoy staying in luxurious hotels because they are consumed with worry and totally pre-occupied about their return flight. These travellers state they don't really relax until they are home again.

In an effort to reassure these passengers the following suggestions should assist greatly.

- Make a list of friends, relatives and business contacts you will be associating with at your destination.
- Leave your hotel or business address and telephone numbers and the date of your return trip.
- Take your mobile phone with you and call home as soon as you arrive.

Flight-related Fears

The fears of those in the second category focus mainly on various aspects of the flight experience, such as the sounds, sensations and movements of the aircraft. For many the anxiety starts from the moment they purchase their flight tickets and continues to increase when packing their bags and saying goodbye to family and friends.

On arrival at the airport their levels of fear intensify as they go through the routine procedures of checking in and waiting in the boarding area for their flight departure call. The fear further increases as they walk down the jetway and board the aeroplane. At this point they feel they have reached the point of no return and there is no escape when the door has closed and the plane taxies out towards the runway. The severest symptoms are experienced with particular regard to the following.

Take-off

Before the flight takes off, the cabin crew is required to demonstrate the on-board safety procedures, which is an official requirement on all flights. Unfortunately, many nervous travellers find this an intimidating sight, making them more nervous and confirming the belief that flying is dangerous. On the other hand, many find it reassuring, seeing the demonstration as evidence of high safety standards.

For many the fear reaches a peak at the moment when take-off is imminent and unavoidable. Nervous passengers describe how they get cramps in their legs as a result of physically applying imaginary brakes to stop the acceleration at take-off. Others describe how they lean forward with all their might and energy to counterbalance the effects of take-off. The sensation of being thrust back into the seat, the roar of the engines, the sounds and movements of the aircraft as it accelerates down the runway at high speed and lifts off into the air, followed by the undercarriage retracting and the flaps being lifted, causes very high anxiety. Many feel the agony of take-off lasts for ever and are very surprised to learn it is usually accomplished in 48–50 seconds. The higher the altitude of the airport, the longer the take-off distance (for example, Johannesburg takes over two minutes). They admit they are totally baffled as to how something as big and heavy as an aeroplane gets off the ground.

When the pilot of a fully laden Boeing 747 pushes the throttles forward to commence take-off, he needs to accelerate to a speed of 180 m.p.h. in order to lift the aircraft off the ground. Most major airports have runways two or three kilometres long to afford sufficient room for the speed-gathering required for take-off. (The sound of tyres bumping over expansion joints can be heard at this stage.) All aircraft have dual controls, dual flight panels and multiple back-up systems in the unlikely event of either one of the pilots taking ill.

After Take-off

A few seconds after take-off, many passengers complain of a floating sensation, as though they are rising out of their seats, accompanied by a strange feeling in their stomach. This can occur as the pilot lowers the nose of the aeroplane and decreases power. The aerodynamics of the plane dictate that the aircraft speed increases, even though the noise of the engines is reduced. All these stages are carried out in practised sequences by the pilots.

Following take-off, the engines are still at full power and noises can be heard, such as the flaps on the wings being retracted and the undercarriage being stored into the wheel bays. The aircraft continues to climb 1,000 feet or more as engine noises can be heard changing to normal. The reduction in engine noise after take-off may be due to noise abatement over built-up areas, but it must be emphasised that the pilot never reduces power below normal. When the plane is banking, some nervous passengers say they continue to thrust their body in the opposite direction to try to counterbalance the turn.

Maurice Yaffe, psychologist, has described how at ground level our sense of orientation is established by gravity and the horizon. All the information we need is acquired from eyes, ears and proprioceptors — the receptors or sense organs located within the tissues of the body. The information furnished by these sensory modalities, in particular from the inner ear and proprioceptors, may be wrongly interpreted and cause anxiety. Yaffe has described how anxiety frequently occurs when frightened passengers avoid looking out the window or close their eyes and try to counter the effects of the aeroplane banking or turning. Over 80 per cent of our input is gleaned from visual cues, so it is not altogether unexpected that when flying as a passenger with the only reference point being a sideways view through the window, feelings of disorientation can occur from misunderstanding these unfamiliar cues.

Motion Sickness

Motion sickness occurs when you are exposed to a real or perceived motion of an unfamiliar nature. The general symptoms include nausea, vomiting, pallor and cold sweating. It is extremely distressing but is a normal reaction to the apparent motion and can be experienced by anyone with a normal sense of balance if they are exposed to the motion indefinitely.

The vestibular apparatus which is located in the ear plays an important role in the detection of this movement and the brain makes comparisons between these signals and the signals obtained from the eyes. As the brain does not get a clear picture, it does everything possible to save us from calamity. As it actually thinks that the body is being poisoned, it therefore ejects all matter from the stomach. That is the reason why we get sick. The most effective way of dealing with motion sickness is to keep your head still and close your eyes. Some medicine is available which can reduce the symptoms and your doctor will advise you on a suitable remedy for this problem.

In-flight Fears

While some nervous passengers are able to relax after take-off, others continue to feel frightened. The fear of unbalancing the aircraft is a major concern. Many are so convinced of this that they are too scared to turn the pages of a book or magazine. Others find it difficult to resist the urge to shout at fellow passengers to stay in their seats and stop moving around. Some passengers never leave their seats for the entire duration of long-haul flights, not even to go to the bathroom! When these passengers learn that the plane is balanced at every stage of the flight from take-off to landing and has many stabilisers to prevent the plane becoming unbalanced, it allays their fear considerably.

The sound of the flight crew call-bell strikes terror in the hearts of many who are convinced this is a private signal between the crew that something serious is amiss. These sounds are signals or a means of communication both for passengers to attract the attention of the cabin crew and for the flight crew to contact one another in various parts of the aeroplane. For example, one single ding of the call-bell is heard when the 'Fasten seat belt' sign is switched on or off in the cabin. Whenever the cabin crew at the front of the cabin need to speak to their colleagues at the rear, two chimes can be heard, indicating that the internal telephone system is in use. If the pilot wishes to speak to the cabin crew, he presses a button in the cockpit which also chimes in the galley area. There is nothing sinister about these in-flight dings. They are a simple, effective communication system used by the crew.

Some passengers admit they never take their eyes off the cabin crew, especially when they go into the cockpit. When they return to the cabin, they anxiously scan their faces for any sign of distress. If they look calm and happy, they feel everything is under control and they can relax. There are those who do not relax until they hear the captain make an announcement with flight details; others sit in dread each time he comes on the public address system, always fearing the worst.

Unfamiliar Engine Noises

Some passengers compensate for the lack of visual cues by focusing their attention on the engine noises heard in the cabin. As passengers don't really know what is or is not normal with regard to the changes in engine noises, this is also a cause of great anxiety. Changes in engine noises can be misunderstood, which can increase feelings of vulnerability and the anticipation of imminent disaster.

One of the features of a phobia is that it involves the appraisal of high-risk factors in a situation that is relatively safe. The anxious individual is on the alert for any indications of danger. Passengers when flying hear a variety of unrecognisable sounds and also experience sensations and movements that are not familiar to them. There are several aircraft noises associated with cruising, descent and landing that worry nervous passengers intensely. All these add to their anxiety.

Cruising

When a plane is flying in level flight it is described as being in the cruise. Passengers generally believe that once the plane is cruising, any change from altitude or change in engine noises means there is a problem. One of the reasons for changing altitude is that when the plane is cruising, fuel is used and the aeroplane becomes lighter. As this occurs the pilot may request changing to a higher altitude to avoid or lessen the effects of turbulence. Another reason for doing this is to conserve fuel. Aircraft flying closer to their ideal altitude are more fuel efficient and therefore more cost efficient. Thus it is more economical to fly higher as the plane's fuel, which constitutes a large part of its weight, is burned off. Slight changes in air-conditioning and engine noises will also be heard during these altitude changes.

Descent

As the flight commences its descent, engine noises will lessen as the pilot reduces power and various high-pitched whines will be heard as devices such as flaps and spoilers on the wings are extended. The undercarriage will be lowered and noise levels increase as the pilot prepares to land.

Passengers sometimes complain of pain in their ears or deafness when the plane is descending. This is usually a temporary inconvenience. There are gases present throughout the body, in the sinuses, the middle ear and the gastrointestinal tract. The middle ear is an air-filled cavity linked to the nose and throat by means of the Eustachian tube. The walls of this tube are soft and the nasal end has a flap valve. During the descent ventilation of the middle ear becomes more difficult because the flap valve can prevent air returning to the middle ear to equalise pressure. The inability to re-establish the normal pressure inside the middle ear can result in pain in the ears.

Normally the sinuses ventilate without trouble. Sinuses are situated above the eyes, in the cheeks and at the back of the nose. In much the same way as the ears, they can vent gas more easily on the ascent than on the descent. However, passengers who suffer from sinusitis, nasal catarrh and colds may have difficulty ventilating their ears on the descent and may experience some pain. It should be pointed out that clinical reports have revealed that heavy smokers are more vulnerable to these symptoms than non-smokers. In order to avoid pain in the ears, the following may be helpful:

- moving your jaw
- yawning
- swallowing
- chewing
- using a good decongestant.

Landing

After touchdown, engine noise increases as the pilot puts the engines into reverse thrust and the brakes are applied, which may cause a grinding sound. Other high-pitched whines are heard as flaps are retracted on the wings. We are all familiar with our car engine noises which vary according to the make and manufacture. Similarly, aircraft engine noises vary according to the type of aircraft, phases of flight and also where you are sitting on board. As mentioned, engine noises are louder at take-off and at various stages of the descent than they are when the plane is in the cruise. Sitting over the wings and at the back is nosier than sitting at the front. Nervous fliers find it hard to understand that the noises they fear are in fact safe, routine sounds associated with the normal operation of the aeroplane. Most passengers do not understand all the noises associated with today's modern jet aircraft. Some find having information about the technical aspects of flying very helpful. This will be dealt with in a later chapter.

Turbulence

Following take-off many victims describe how they sit in terror anticipating the thought of flying through turbulence at any moment. The mere mention of the word 'turbulence' is enough to strike horror in the hearts of the majority of fearful fliers.

When turbulence occurs, they genuinely fear it will damage the aeroplane or that it will cause the plane to spiral out of control. They visualise the pilots struggling at the controls to maintain its balance. They firmly believe that if they are frightened, then the pilot must be too, especially when he announces 'We are experiencing some unexpected turbulence', and they think, 'If he wasn't expecting it, what hope have we of surviving!' Each time they confront turbulence, they believe they are dicing with death.

Numerous former aerophobics have said that they had pains in their arms for days after flying through turbulence, the result of gripping the arm-rest of their seat when making strenuous efforts to counteract their perceived lack of balance of the aircraft. 'White-knuckle' passengers are those who insist they feel secure when they grab the seat-back in front of them, the arm-rest of their seat or grab the hand of the passenger sitting next to them. Without realising it, they are creating more tension in the muscles along their arms, across their chest and upper back, which in turn affects their breathing and invariably leads to an increase in distressing anxiety symptoms.

A good point to remember is that when a pilot makes a flight, he is not going out on a death wish and under no circumstances will he do anything to endanger your life or his own. The sensation of being randomly jolted upwards, downwards and sideways is not within your normal earthbound experience, so you feel vulnerable because of the unpredictable and unexpected movements of the aircraft, which you are not in a position to control. As passengers, you cannot predict when turbulence will occur or how long it will last, nor can you do anything to stop it.

The Nature of Turbulence

Earth is surrounded by an ocean of air and mankind could not survive without it. However, because we cannot see it, we are inclined to forget that air is predominantly a fluid which is constantly in motion. Air is constantly shifting and moves in three dimensions: vertically, horizontally and diagonally. Turbulence is the disorganised movement of air. Air moving fast becomes wind; steady wind becomes gusty when moving across uneven terrain such as mountains, trees, built-up areas and high-rise buildings. Wind cannot move through these features, so it is forced to rise, and in doing so disturbs the air already in place, causing it too to move. When a mass of cold air meets warm air, in view of the fact that cold air is heavier, it dislodges the warm air, resulting in warm air rising. This in turn produces rain and also sets air in motion. The sun warms the earth and causes moisture to evaporate and air to rise. As this air rises, it displaces other air.

It doesn't always happen in this sequence, but these are the factors involved. Ships couldn't sail if there weren't any oceans; equally aeroplanes couldn't fly without the element of air. Planes can fly quite safely through choppy or disturbed air just as ships can safely sail through rough seas. All new modern airliners have winglets on their wing tips, which greatly reduce the effects of turbulence.

Clear Air Turbulence

Clear air turbulence, which is very rare and often unforeseeable, occurs at high altitudes when two air streams moving at different speeds converge. Rough disturbed air or turbulence results where they meet. Similarly, if you visualise two fast-moving streams flowing down a mountain side at different speeds, the surface of the water, where they merge with the calm, slower moving water of a river, becomes choppy. Pilots are fully aware that passengers find turbulence uncomfortable and in order to minimise their discomfort, they will seek permission from air traffic control to change altitude or fly around it.

Air pockets

There are no 'holes in the sky': air pockets are a fantasy description of turbulence. There is no such thing as an empty space in the atmosphere. When a plane is flying through turbulence it is always flying through air. Imagine yourself walking up a flight of steps in the dark. You take that last step which isn't there and you feel the 'imaginary step' to be much steeper than the real ones. You may have fallen as a result of taking that imaginary step and yet you only raised your foot the same height as for a previous step. Perception can play tricks on your imagination.

The cockpit altimeter indicates how much an aeroplane moves when flying through turbulence and, according to the majority of pilots, the variations are very small. There is a turbulence scale that ranges from zero to 10. Zero on the scale signifies that there is no turbulence. 10 denotes extremely heavy turbulence, which is never encountered because it is illegal to route an aircraft into such conditions. The average level of turbulence is around three which, although it is uncomfortable, is not regarded as dangerous and cannot harm you or the aeroplane.

Return to Your Seats and Fasten Your Seatbelts

When the captain or cabin crew makes this announcement it is in the interests of safety and comfort, not because of danger. The aircraft is structurally sound and has been designed and strenuously tested to ensure it can withstand the stress of turbulence. Turbulence will not unbalance the plane. A plane has various stabilisers and remains balanced throughout all phases of flight, including flying through turbulent air. Pilots have advance information from radar and air traffic control regarding weather en route. In most conditions the plane is on autopilot when flying through turbulence. The autopilot can sense any changes that are occurring in the air currents and can make the necessary changes to compensate accordingly. Notwithstanding this, pilots are trained to the highest possible standards and are perfectly capable of flying the plane in all types of situations, including turbulence.

Turbulence can also be experienced at sea and on the ground. The effects of flying through turbulence is similar to sailing across rough seas or driving across a cobble-stoned road or a road with potholes at 30 m.p.h. A racing car driver explained that turbulence during a flight was the least of his worries, as he had frequently experienced driving through turbulent air on the ground when competing in races. He explained that when he stayed on the track behind a car which was already cutting a channel through the air at high speed, as long as he followed the car in front directly he had a smooth drive, but as soon as he crossed the slipstream of the car in front of him, he felt the full impact of being tossed across the racetrack due to disturbed air at ground surface.

The best way to deal with turbulence is to keep your seatbelt fastened throughout the flight. Make an effort to resist the temptation to grip the arm-rest or seat-back in front of you, try to relax and go with the flow or movements of the aeroplane and remind yourself of the nature of turbulence. Tell yourself that it is uncomfortable but not dangerous.

Wind Shear

Wind shear occurs when the direction and speed of wind changes dramatically over a short distance and in a brief timespan. Wind shear rarely occurs at high altitudes. It is reassuring to know that aircraft manufacturers have developed and installed on-board wind shear detection and avoidance systems into some new jetliners, such as the Airbus A330 and the Boeing 737-300. In addition, pilots receive instruction in coping with wind shear and if this condition occurs in the landing configuration, it is mandatory to report it immediately to air traffic control. Pilots are trained to recognise such conditions in a flight simulator and have learned how to deal with it appropriately.

Flying Through Thunderstorms

Pilots check the weather before each and every flight and at every airport there is a meteorological self-briefing office that pinpoints the motion of clouds and the various build-ups that cause a thunderstorm. Not all cumulus nimbus clouds, which are called CBs, turn out to be active thunderstorms, and even the largest, darkest cloud in the sky can be benign. In other words, it could just be full of rain. Once the heavy rain falls, the large cloud dissipates and the classic anvil shape is produced.

In modern jet planes, weather radar is located in the nose cone of the aircraft which shows the pilot precisely where the storms exist. Air traffic control can ascertain the severity of storms and can reroute the flight to a different altitude. It is for this reason that pilots will always give active CBs a wide berth and either fly over or around them to avoid stormy conditions.

Passengers on board an aircraft are often frightened of a lightning strike. These are very rare and are usually accompanied by bright flashes and loud thunderclaps. Lightning causes minimal, if any, damage to aeroplanes. In the highly unlikely event that a plane is struck by lightning, the pilot will land at the nearest airport to check if any damage has been caused. Pilots generally avoid thunderstorms and at altitude commercial aircraft must stay 20 miles from the nucleus of a thunderstorm. An aeroplane is a completely bonded metal conductor and reacts to lightning according to the principle of a Faraday cage. The scientist Michael Faraday found that if electricity is put through a metal box or cage, irrespective of the strength or intensity of the voltage, items inside the metal box or cage are completely protected from the electricity. Based on this principle, the design of the aircraft ensures that static electricity is dispelled very quickly. Lightning injures and kills hundreds of people annually on the ground and in their own homes, but passengers are always safe on board an aeroplane, whether it is on the ground or in the air during a thunderstorm. Incidentally, the most dangerous place to be in a lightning storm is sheltering under a tree or on a golf course, where if you ground your club you automatically become a lightning conductor.

Fog

Poor visibility, heavy rain and low cloud can also influence an anxious passenger's decision whether to take a flight or not. Flight schedules which are disrupted due to such weather conditions occur mainly because the aircraft or the specific airport does not have the necessary automatic landing equipment or technology to make a landing in poor visibility. In order to achieve this type of landing, the runway must be equipped with an electronic glide slope to make an instrument landing possible. The on-board equipment consists of a computerised automatic pilot which locks on to a radio beam relayed by the ground aerial of the instrument landing system. The autopilot flies the aircraft along this beam to touchdown, while regulating the engine speed and the angle of approach. Not all aircraft or runways are equipped with this advanced technology, which in avionic terms is regarded as a CAT III approach.

In poor visibility, pilots adhere to a 'minima criteria' and will not land or take off unless a section of the runway is visible, which is called runway visual range (RVR). Subsequently, as fog is a 'drifting phenomenon' from ground level to an unknown height, pilots do not take off or land in such conditions, as fog could block the RVR and the pilots would not have the minimal references required. That is why pilots nominate alternate airports en route. Nowadays, thanks to the development of sophisticated instrumentation on aircraft and runway categories at many major international airports, flights can land and take off safely in weather conditions that until recently would have closed the airport and caused the flight to divert elsewhere.

Safety

It is a fact of life that accidents do happen with loss of life and they are all tragic, whether at sea, by rail, in the air or on the roadways, irrespective of whether loss of life is single or multiple. It is for this reason that every aircraft is equipped with a cockpit flight recorder, which tapes the pilots' radio conversations during each flight, and a flight data apparatus which is familiarly known to us as the 'black box'.

Ask any pilot what the most dangerous aspect of flying is and he will probably answer 'the drive from my home to the airport'. It is a proven fact that more fatalities occur on the roads than in the air. It is a sobering thought for air travellers that more people are killed on the roads every day than are killed in the air every year. In the United States a fully loaded Boeing 747 would have to crash every day with no survivors to equal the number of road fatalities.

The possibility of being killed or injured in an aeroplane disaster is a very strong reason for flight-related fear or not flying at all. Yet when the safety record of air transportation is taken into account, it is clear that it is a far safer form of transport.

Some Statistics

Thanks to the high standards of air safety worldwide, flight-related accidents are extremely rare in proportion to the number of aircraft flying all over the world every second of the day. For example, there are now eight major international airlines operating as members of a oneworld global alliance. In their first year of amalgamation they operated approximately two million flights, with a oneworld airline departure taking place somewhere around the world every 14 seconds.

Most air travellers are familiar with Boeing aeroplanes; on a recent trip to Seattle to visit the Boeing Aircraft Company, I was advised that a Boeing airliner takes off or lands somewhere in the world every five seconds. These jetliners carry 2.7 million passengers every day on vacation or to business meetings all over the world. There are literally millions of people being transported safely all over the world, every day of the year, by various aeroplanes in addition to Boeing jetliners. All these figures should help reinforce the fact that air transport is in a league of its own and is unquestionably one of the safest forms of transportation known to mankind.

Flight Personnel

THE AVIATION AUTHORITY OF the country in which an aircraft is registered, for example the Federal Aviation Administration (FAA) in the United States, the Civil Aviation Authority (CAA) in the United Kingdom and the Irish Aviation Authority (IAA) in Ireland, establishes and enforces strict air safety standards for airlines and air crews. In addition to the aircraft manufacturers' flight tests, further investigations are conducted to specifications set by these authorities.

The pilots carry out tests in order to confirm that the aircraft can function safely and reliably in manoeuvres far in excess of normal limits. When all the investigations have been completed and all the relevant authorities are satisfied, the obligatory Certificate of Airworthiness is granted by the relevant national aviation authority. On delivery of a new aeroplane, airlines continue to perform further tests and flight checks, in some cases arranging trial flights on the routes to be used before introducing it into passenger service.

Aircraft Maintenance Engineers

All aircraft engineers undergo rigorous training and must pass certain examinations to obtain their qualifications and licence to practise from the aviation authority of the country in which they work.

The first priority of an airline is its aircraft safety. When a flight lands at its home base or a faraway destination, one of the first ground staff personnel on board is an engineer who asks for the technical log. Any problems, technical or otherwise, which the cockpit or cabin crew want checking or rectifying are recorded in the technical log. These can range from a blocked sink, a seat-back that needs adjusting or any system that the captain wants checking or replacing. When the engineer has finished working on the problem, he confirms that it has been satisfactorily rectified. In addition to this, the engineer also carries out a series of essential pre-flight checks before the plane takes off again.

Aircraft must be serviced and maintained by authorised procedures and engineers perform a structured series of ongoing, detailed checks, which are of increasing complexity and duration. Depending on the aircraft size, type and manufacture, many aircraft must undergo a comprehensive check after 50–60 flying hours, with further and more detailed checks after 300–600 flying hours. A full overhaul, which can take approximately one month, is carried out after 3,600 hours of flying time. After 10 years of approximately 25,000 flying hours, the aeroplane is totally stripped down and every single part of every system and component is meticulously examined, using sophisticated technology and equipment to check for signs of flaws, cracks or corrosion. The wings, landing gear and fuel tanks are inspected inside and out, in addition to toilets and galleys, and all other relevant systems are examined and replaced as required. This in-depth check takes many weeks to complete. When the work has been completed to the satisfaction of the supervisory engineers, the aircraft undergoes further inspection, including a test flight, before being put back into passenger service again.

Air Traffic Control

Every second of the day a considerable number of aeroplanes are airborne at different speeds, in different directions and at different altitudes. The main task of air traffic control is to monitor this traffic and ensure a safe separation distance at all times.

As will be further explained in Chapter 6, the flight crew check in about an hour and a half before a flight. They complete a flight plan which contains information regarding the aircraft registration, flight number, aircraft type, time of flight departure, number of passengers on board, which route to be flown, altitude preferred, fuel on board, weather expected en route, destination, total flight time and all other relevant information, including alternate airports. These are used in the event of bad weather at the destination airport. Irrespective of whether it is a two-seater light aircraft going on a short flight or a wide-bodied Airbus or Boeing 747 flying long-haul, the crew must always file a flight plan giving all these important details. It is then filed with air traffic control for onward distribution.

The Control Tower

The control tower is the nerve centre of an airport, which in Ireland is administered by the Irish Aviation Authority. The control tower plays a vital role in air safety and is responsible for ensuring the safe, efficient and expeditious movement of air traffic within its control zone. Air traffic services provide and direct specific services essential for the safe navigation of air traffic within the airspace for which the Irish government has custody. The airspace ranges from approximately 30 miles east of the eastern Irish coast-line to approximately 200 miles west of the Atlantic coastline and approximately 250 miles from north Donegal to approximately 200 miles south of the country. The vertical limit of the airspace is from ground level with no specified upper limit. Air traffic is regulated in accordance with standards established internationally.

Duties of an Air Traffic Controller

The duties of an air traffic control officer are diverse and broad ranging. They give instructions and clearances to pilots to affirm that separation according to international standards is maintained between controlled aircraft. They also give advice and information on weather conditions, runway conditions, serviceability of nav-igation aids and traffic information to non-schedule flights. Since the nature of air traffic varies between each of the services providing aerodrome control, area control or approach control, the procedure by which separation is assured varies considerably.

Radar is the major instrument employed by air traffic con-trollers. This allows continuous monitoring of an aircraft's position, flight level and direction of flight. Radio and radar are vital instruments for maintaining a safe separation between aircraft, ensuring their safe and efficient progress en route to their destination. Radar corresponds automatically with the transponder on board each aircraft, which then responds by giving the identity of the aircraft and its altitude. The radar system calculates the position and direction of the aircraft. This information is viewed by the controllers, who then give essential information to the cockpit crew in order to direct them safely along their flight path.

Control towers in all major airports have two control centres: the visual or ground control at the top of the tower and the main control centre, which is separate from ground control. Ground controllers handle the initial communication from the aircraft on the ground, giving them clearance to start up their engines and move away from the departure terminal gate. They then pass them over to the tower controller, who will already be fully apprised of their flight plan, filed earlier by the pilot. He guides them to the active runway in use, informs them of any incoming traffic and eventually clears them for take-off.

As soon as the aircraft leaves the ground, the tower controller transfers the flight to another controller in the control centre. Here, the controller, using radar, will observe and supervise the flight path of the aircraft as it leaves the runway, takes off and joins a particular airway. Airways are designated navigational channels through the airspace connecting major control centres in different countries, where all aircraft are allocated specific altitudes and horizontal separation distances.

Safe vertical separation involves directing aircraft to fly at different levels, which guarantees they are flying at a minimum vertical distance which has been measured in feet. The minimum separation stipulated by international agreement varies, depending on the altitude of the aircraft.

Air Traffic

Controllers constantly monitor distance separation to allow more than one aircraft to fly along the same route at the same altitude. They are fully advised regarding the speeds at which the aircraft are flying and consistently study the separation distance to confirm that it is maintained and is not being encroached upon. The distance between aircraft depends on the type of aircraft and where the aircraft is flying.

Using surveillance radar which identifies each aircraft and shows its speed, position and altitude, the controller will continue to monitor the aircraft while in that country's airspace. As the aeroplane travels from one country to another, the control responsibility is handed over accordingly. The air traffic control service is of the same standard across all international borders, ensuring the safe continuity of air travel across the globe.

The Pilot

'Good morning, ladies and gentlemen, this is your captain speaking.' The voice of the captain or co-pilot on the public address system always ensures the attention of the passengers on board. This is the voice of the person in charge of the entire flight and also the person who fearful fliers have no option but to trust. Firstly, they do know what they are doing. Secondly, there is absolutely no truth in the myth that pilots' personalities are daredevil and gung-ho. Thirdly, and more importantly, they are very dedicated professionals, selected on the basis of maturity, stability and qualities such as leadership and responsibility, among others.

The qualifications and training of the pilot is a source of real concern for many. You can rest assured that they are highly skilled people, the majority of whom have attained qualifications in academic and technical studies. Their qualifications, training and ongoing supervision for the duration of their career meets the highest possible standard of any profession, as you are now going to learn.

There are various routes to joining an airline, such as a cadetship whereby the respective airline arranges the training of the student pilot. Others who have already completed a dedicated course of training in a flying school and achieved a commercial pilot's licence may apply to an airline. This is called the direct entry. More may come from a military background or already have flying experience with another airline.

Following the initial selection for working with an airline, suitable applicants undergo an aptitude test. Those attaining the required standard are then called to attend preliminary interviews and an assessment is made regarding their overall suitability. If successful, they are called for further interviews and are given a battery of psychological tests to evaluate their aptitude and stability and take part in group exercises. Candidates who are selected must undergo a rigorous medical examination, following which decisions on final selections are made. A high standard of physical health is essential. Chest X-rays, ECG and EEG examinations are compulsory, along with ENT, hearing and visual examinations.

No other group of professionals come under the same scrutiny and supervision as a pilot. Irrespective of their years of service, they are required to understand the working and operations of any new computer developments in the airline industry. Throughout their career, they are subjected to regular checks to test their flying skills, and of even greater significance, they are examined in the flight simulator on how they perform in response to an emergency situation. This is to ensure that their reactions to a set of catastrophes, more than they are ever likely to encounter in their flying career, can be practised and evaluated. Though such flight emergencies are rare, repeat training sessions ensure that pilots maintain their proficiency in handling such unique events.

Pilots are 'line checked' regularly. They never know when they are going to be checked on a flight. A line-check pilot simply arrives unexpectedly on board the aeroplane and announces to the crew that he is going to carry out a line check. This consists of observing how the crew operates both individually and together as a team.

The health of the pilot is under scrutiny throughout his or her career. Senior pilots over the age of 40 must undergo a full medical check every six months, including an ECG, by the airline's designated doctor. Pilots under 40 have a medical check once a year.

An additional health precaution is a stipulation that when flying, the captain and co-pilot must always eat different meals, which safeguards against the possibility of food poisoning. There are also strict guidelines specified by the airlines with regard to the amount of alcohol a pilot may consume on a weekly basis and prior to taking out a flight.

Pilots cannot achieve the rank of captain until they have flown as first officer and promotion usually depends on seniority. On board the aeroplane the captain has ultimate authority and full responsibility for the aircraft. He makes all the relevant decisions regarding the safety and well-being of passengers and crew. A captain's normal retirement age is 60.

Cabin Crew

The cabin crew are the major link between the airline and the passengers. No two flights are ever the same and their skills are constantly on call for attending to passengers' various needs. Not many people realise that in the course of a transatlantic flight a cabin crew member can walk in excess of twelve miles. Their workload is wide and varied, from looking after elderly passengers to supervising young children, known in aviation terms as UMS (unaccompanied minors).

It has already been noted that the cabin crew are very important people in the estimation of fearful fliers who frequently remark, 'No matter what engine noises upset me or turbulence we fly through, I never take my eyes off the stewards or stewardesses. If they appear calm and unconcerned, it helps reassure me that everything is all right.'

Aspiring candidates must be at least 18 years of age, have a good educational background and a pleasant, confident manner. A neat, well-groomed appearance is important, along with good communication skills. Fluency in a foreign language and nursing skills are an advantage and applicants need to enjoy working as a team.

Successful candidates then undergo a comprehensive training course which lasts approximately eight weeks. They undergo safety training and are required to pass examinations on safety procedures which are set by the Irish Aviation Authority. Instruction is also given in personal development, grooming, effective customer service and communication skills, all services for the duration of the flight and making public address announcements.

On all flights there is a senior cabin crew member who is in charge and on all wide-bodied aeroplanes this crew member is referred to as a cabin manager or purser. They designate specific work duties to each cabin crew member, liaise with ground personnel and the captain, deal with complaints and supervise the smooth flow of in-flight services. The cabin crew are very understanding and caring people whose charm and good nature add to the smooth running of a flight. They are always there to assist their passengers in any way possible and they will always look after a nervous passenger.

CHAPTER FIVE

They Really do Fly

By J. P. Crangle

IT IS A SOURCE OF excitement and awe to see a large Boeing 747 or an Airbus A330 take off into the air. Many people wonder how something so enormous can even get off the ground.

Just as a fish swims through water, we are completely submerged in air, which analytically is described as a flowing mass. This flowing mass is now referred to as a fluid by eminent scientists worldwide. When we look around us, we can easily see that birds, insects and even bats can fly, and if this fluid wasn't there, it would be totally impossible for them to do so. What all these creatures have in common are their wings, without which flight would be impossible.

The theory of flight has been expounded from very early times and even though people believed that the world was flat, they also accepted that

- weight kept them on the ground
- thrust forced them forward
- drag held them back.

These became known as the common forces and by the middle of the fifteenth century great men such as Leonardo da Vinci were developing these theories further.

During the nineteenth century many famous Europeans further augmented the various theories and a fourth force was ratified, called 'lift'. Just as the early philosophers understood weight, thrust and drag, we should not have any great problems understanding these forces either, as they are all self-explanatory. So let us look at this fourth force called lift.

Lift was widely studied by the Wright brothers, who were originally bicycle mechanics, and they accepted all previous scientific findings. They solely developed the steering mechanism that is still used today in all modern aeroplanes. This of course was one of the greatest forward steps in aviation history and in order to achieve such an advancement, the Wright brothers departed for Kitty Hawk in the Carolinas during the last decade of the nineteenth century and in the high winds watched various birds in flight. With great attention to detail, they recorded how certain feathers on the birds' wings protruded and retracted when turning, climbing and descending and they applied this to the wings of their very own aircraft. In 1903 these gentlemen made their historic flight, thus proving to the world that it was now possible to take a heavier-than-air machine from the ground to the air and bring it back to the ground again. They had achieved the first controlled flight.

Look at this fluid that surrounds you. You can feel it when you move your hands up and down and you can definitely experience it when you are out running. Even though you might have the wind at your back, you will always have the wind in your face when moving forward. This is called the relative airflow. We live on a planet with an atmosphere which is subject to climatic change and this is very evident on a windy night. If you want to be correct, instead of saying, 'It's a windy night tonight', you should say, 'It's an air travelling fast night tonight.' What you are experiencing at times like this is the movement of the fluid. This fluid or air is approximately four-fifths nitrogen and one-fifth oxygen and, to be exact, there are also an insignificant number of inert gases present. All these put together form one of our greatest elements. Unlike water the fluid cannot be seen, but it can be weighed and measured. For instance, a cubic foot of air weighs about 1$\frac{1}{3}$ ounces.

Now that we know that we are surrounded by a fluid, let us look more closely at the wings, which essentially are the most important part of an aircraft. Without wings an aeroplane could not fly. Contrary to the general perception, wings are not stuck on to the sides of an aircraft but in fact are constructed in one section and the cabin (or the fuselage, as it is known) is built either above or below the wings. In other words, the wings, which are in one piece, run right through the aircraft.

The wings are designed so that the relative airflow speeds up as it passes over the upper surface, thus creating a lower static pressure and an upward aerodynamic force. This might sound

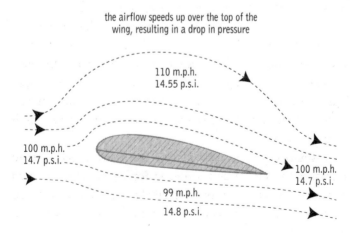

the airflow speeds up over the top of the
wing, resulting in a drop in pressure

110 m.p.h.
14.55 p.s.i.

100 m.p.h.
14.7 p.s.i.

100 m.p.h.
14.7 p.s.i.

99 m.p.h.

14.8 p.s.i.

highly technical and complicated, but put simply, what happens is that the pressure on top of the wing decreases below the normal atmospheric pressure and this produces an upward force.

If there is a decrease in pressure, there must also be a corresponding increase in pressure elsewhere, and this occurs below the wings. The high pressure generated is very small but does create a slight upward dynamic force which experts maintain is very insignificant. That is why engines, mountings, aerials, struts, supports and armaments in military aircraft are all housed under the wings so that the top is kept clean and free from all obstructions. This upward movement created by the low pressure on top of the wing is called lift and is the principal force of flight.

Remember that the Wright brothers fully accepted this theory and clarification from past masters and went on to successfully construct the aircraft steering equipment that is still used today, so we can also accept this knowledge unequivocally. You can ascertain what lift is by putting your hand out through the open window of a fast-moving car. As you incline the palm of your hand slightly upwards, the airflow passing over it generates low pressure on the top of your hand and forces it upwards. Exactly the same thing happens with the wings of an aircraft.

If we use an office fan to simulate the airflow, curve the leading edge of a piece of paper so that it resembles the front of a wing. Holding it below the fan, slowly move it up into the flow, making sure that the airflow only passes over the top of the paper and not underneath. Once again low pressure is created on top of the paper and the remaining piece of paper raises itself horizontal to the flow.

A similar experiment can also be created by using water to represent the airflow and a large spoon. If the spoon is held downwards and the back of it is gently brought into contact with the flow of water from a tap, the water will pull the spoon into

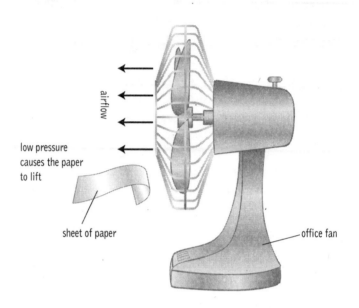

airflow

low pressure
causes the paper
to lift

sheet of paper

office fan

the flow instead of pushing it away. Here again the fluid, this time water instead of air, is flowing around the shape of the spoon, which is almost identical to the top of a wing, causing a reduction in pressure. This drop in pressure is the same as the reduction of pressure on the top of an aircraft's wing and consequently generates exactly the same lifting effect. This experiment is well worth doing as we are using an alloy which is heavier than air, and you will be surprised at the force with which the spoon is pulled into the jet of water.

As soon as the aeroplane begins to move over the ground, low pressure immediately begins to form above its wings. A point is

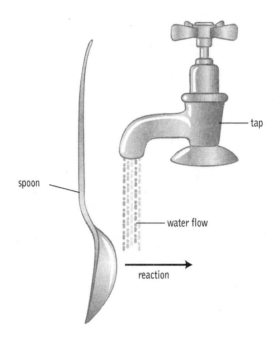

reached as it speeds down the runway where the low pressure is so great, lift equals the all-up weight of the aircraft and the plane has no option but to take off into the air. One of the most reassuring things is that while the plane is in a forward movement, the low pressure above the aircraft's wings is completely self-induced and never goes away. It remains in place at all times and has nothing to do with the engines. Due to this lifting effect, in the unlikely event of an engine failure, the plane would not fall out of the sky but would glide gradually downwards. Again, let us marvel at the space shuttle, which is the greatest glider ever built. This vehicle returns to Earth without any engine assistance

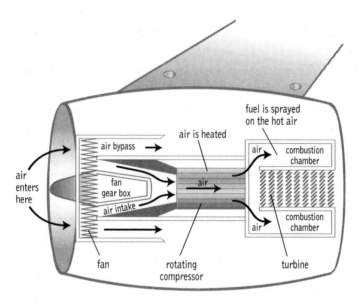

whatsoever. It relies completely for its trajectory on the lift that is generated on top of its wings. Now we have established that there are four basic forces, namely weight, thrust, drag and lift.

The gas turbine (or the jet engine, as it is generally known) consists of a tube or shaft divided into three main sections. Starting at the front there is the compressor, followed by the combustion chambers and finally at the back the turbines. Air is sucked into the front of the engine by a fan. Surplus air escapes by means of a bypass duct. The air which is sucked in by the fan passes through a rotating compressor and in doing so becomes very hot and is forced into the combustion chambers, where it is sprayed with fuel and explodes. The tremendous heat that is generated expands the air, which becomes a gas and moves at great speeds through the narrow pipes to the blades of the turbine wheels. This causes the turbines to rotate and the plane is driven forward. In the 1950s this very simple type of engine transformed the entire airline industry.

As is often the case in aviation history, this basic idea was not a new one. The engine was just another practical example of Newton's law — that every action has an equal and opposite reaction. Blueprints for a type of gas turbine go back as far as the late eighteenth century, but independent results both in Germany and Britain yielded more important discoveries in the early twentieth century and the first jet aeroplane flew in Germany in 1939. It did not go into operation as a fighter aircraft until the very last days of World War Two. The development of this aircraft came too late to have any effect on the result of the war.

Since the mid-1950s the jet engine has not changed very much. With the exception of the gear box, which enhances the intake fan and the rotating compressor, the engine has very few other moving parts. This means of course that there are fewer vibrations and therefore it runs much more smoothly than any other type of engine previously developed.

Look at the entire aeroplane as it sits on the airport apron or the ramp waiting for its passengers before departure. This is where the forces play their part. The aircraft's major distinctive feature is its wings. The very size of the aircraft keeps it on the ground and this is referred to as weight. When airborne, the undercarriage and flaps are retracted in order to reduce drag, which is always kept to a minimum. Finally, we see the engines, which can be positioned under the wings at the rear of the aircraft or even in the tail or rudder, and these provide the necessary thrust to sustain flight. The rudder is the large upright section at the back of the plane which steers it through the air, just as a boat has a rudder to steer it through water.

With all the passengers on board and all formalities completed, the pilot taxies forward to the take-off runway. This movement is another positive proof of how solid the air around us really is, as there is absolutely no connection from the engines to the wheels.

The spinning turbines within the engines simply bite into the air, thus pulling the entire weight of the aircraft across the ground.

When the pilot lines his aircraft up on the runway and receives take-off clearance from air traffic control, he eases the throttles forward. The aeroplane speeds down the runway and with its engines at full power it accelerates to a predetermined speed. For the aircraft to take off, the thrust must be greater than the drag and the lift that occurs on top of its wings must be greater than its weight. When these four forces act together, the aeroplane has no option but to take off and climb into the air when the pilot eases back on the control column.

The only difference between the flight of the Wright brothers and the flight of a Super Boeing 747 or an Airbus A330 is technology. There is no doubt about it, they really do fly.

CHAPTER SIX

The Pilot's Day
By J. P. Crangle

THE COCKPIT CREW ALWAYS assemble about one and a half hours prior to the departure time and today they are taking a domestic flight from Dublin to Cork. The duration of this short flight is only 30 minutes, but that doesn't matter as the same preparations go into this flight as would go into a long-haul flight, for example, from Shannon Airport, Ireland to JFK Airport, New York.

On arrival the captain meets his first officer and they spend the next 30 minutes checking all the information supplied to them by flight operations. They go through every detail and gather as much data as possible. They examine everything carefully, not always accepting the positive hypothesis, and they cross-check and verify what has been given to them. This is called situational awareness. In the self-briefing meteorological office they check the weather between Dublin and Cork and also at alternative airports. In the event of bad weather they check all the minimum requirements and also select an alternative airport, just in case they have to divert. The ideal situation would be to select an alternative airport with different runway headings to the airport of arrival so as to compensate for crosswinds. Ireland is very fortunate in having Shannon International Airport on its Atlantic coastline. This is the transatlantic hub for Aer Lingus and the last major airport in Western Europe.

Having selected Shannon as an alternative, the flight crew makes sure that they have sufficient fuel to get from Dublin to Cork and onward to Shannon if necessary. Fuel shortage would never be a problem on a flight of such a short duration as this. Nevertheless, the quantity of fuel is always checked by various personnel at every out-station before every departure. An alternative airport is selected not just because of weather conditions alone — it could happen that the runway at Cork might be blocked or out of use for numerous reasons. In such an unlikely event, the aeroplane would always divert to a major airport. The captain would radio ahead and liaise with the appropriate airport ground authority in order to ensure that his passengers would have suitable overland transport to continue to their destinations without too much inconvenience. Once cargo is loaded, the total take-off weight is calculated and the aircraft is balanced and trimmed accordingly.

During the next 30 minutes most of the passengers would have checked in and are starting to board. This data is relayed by computer to operations, and this is transcribed to the ship's manifest, together with any other relative information. Strangely enough, even in today's terminology the aircraft is still referred to as a ship. The captain thoroughly examines all documents and at the same time the first officer rechecks all other available airport ground maintenance information of importance to the flight. Needless to say, weather is one of the most important factors of any flight, so it is the topic of conversation with other pilots in the briefing room, particularly with those who have just flown the route.

It is now time for the pilots to leave Operations and board the aeroplane, where they meet the senior steward or stewardess, and before sitting comfortably into the cockpit one of them carries out the mandatory external inspection. This consists of looking at everything within arm's length, including wheels, tyres, struts, tail section and visually checking the navigation lights, wings and fuselage. As this is a most important procedure, a considerable amount of time is allocated to this duty. Meanwhile, the other pilot examines and checks everything inside the cockpit. Within 15 minutes from take-off, when the pilots are comfortably seated, they perform an extensive start-up check. They mandatorily work in tandem, going through the pre-flight checklist with one 'calling out' and the other 'calling check' before moving on to the next item, for example, 'Brakes secure — check' 'Flaps 20 degrees — check' and so on.

All navigational aids are then set and identified for this short flight, and the Dublin VOR beacon and the Cork VOR beacon are programmed into the computer, with additional navigational fixes taken from the Killiney NDB directly to the Clonmel NDB and onward to Cork Airport. VOR stands for very high frequency omnidirectional range and NDB stands for non-directional beacon. The most important instrument on board is the compass and other standard equipment includes the artificial horizon, the turn and slip indicator, the altimeter, the direction indicator, the air-speed indicator and the distance measuring equipment (DME). All these are housed in a modern, sophisticated, computerised panel and at this point all back-up systems are also activated and checked.

Meanwhile, at operations an airline dispatcher completes a flight plan on behalf of the captain. This contains information relating to the type of aircraft, the wake turbulence, on-board equipment, the departure aerodrome, the departure time, the cruising speed, the cruising level, the route, the destination aerodrome, the duration of the flight, the alternate aerodromes, the fuel endurance and the number of persons on board. Nothing is left to chance and further information, such as emergency radios and survival equipment, right down to the number of lifejackets, is also included on this document. This plan is then filed with air traffic control.

When all the passengers are on board, another dispatching official, commonly referred to in aviation terms as the 'redcap', hands the captain all the final details of the flight that have just been generated by the computer. This includes the various acceleration speeds and the exact airspeed at rotation point, which is the point of take-off and climb. The pilots would have previously completed a manual calculation in order to cross-check and verify these figures. The senior cabin attendant verifies a head count of all the passengers and crew on board and reports the number to the captain, who checks his manifest accordingly. After the redcap leaves the aircraft, the doors are securely closed. It can be clearly seen that all personnel work together as a team.

On every flight, except those that are internationally agreed, the registration letters on the side and on the wings of the aircraft are the ship's call sign or registration number. In our case the registration letters are EI-JPC, so when the captain is ready to make his first radio call to air traffic control he says, 'Dublin Ground, good afternoon. Echo India Juliet Pappa Charlie requesting start-up and push back.'

The ATC ground traffic controller replies, 'Good afternoon Pappa Charlie, start-up approved. Call for push when ready, QNH 1013.'

The conversation is polished and dynamic and pilot and controller work together in close accord. The QNH is the current barometric pressure for the particular region the aircraft is flying through. (The duties of air traffic control have already been explained in Chapter 4.)

As aeroplanes do not use reverse thrust, a vehicle called a 'tug' pushes it clear of the boarding gate and any other aircraft that may be in the vicinity. When clear, the pilot gently eases the throttles forward and the aeroplane taxies across the ramp to the take-off runway, which today is runway one-zero. All runways have magnetic headings, so this runway at Dublin Airport runs from west to east on a magnetic heading of 100 degrees. There are still many checks which the pilots carry out before lining up the aircraft on the runway. Just before take-off the captain welcomes the passengers on board, advising them of the flight duration, the route he is about to take and the weather at the destination. Finally, he requests passengers to bring their seat-backs to the upright position and to ensure that their seatbelts are securely fastened, which is of the utmost importance. The ground controller confirms the 'route clearance' with the cockpit crew before instructing them to contact the tower frequency for 'departure clearance'. All this is duly acknowledged by one of the pilots, with a confirmation reply from the ground controller: 'Read back correct.'

On contacting the tower frequency the same courteous radio procedure is repeated, only this time the controller tells the captain to climb to 4,000 feet after take-off. This command is acknowledged explicitly and the captain lines his aircraft up on runway one-zero and waits for the final take-off clearance from Dublin Tower Control: 'Pappa Charlie cleared for take-off, runway one-zero, with a right turn out to Killiney, QNH 1013.'

Once again the captain acknowledges this clearance word for word and eases the throttles forward to full power. The engines develop so much thrust that the aircraft uses less than half the available length of this 2.5 kilometre runway and continues to accelerate after take-off and climbs at an approximate angle of 16 degrees. As the aircraft climbs through 2,000 feet, it commences a gentle 30 degree turn to the right over Dublin Bay. It then ascends to 4,000 feet as it approaches its first reporting point at Killiney. When it reaches Killiney, it is cleared onwards to an altitude between 15,000 and 20,000 feet, which is the normal flight level for this short journey.

At this stage of the flight the captain engages the automatic pilot, which can fly and hold the plane on its intended heading and this affords the pilots more time to supervise the various dials and instruments within the cockpit. En route the pilot transfers frequencies to Dublin Radar before contacting Shannon Control, which is responsible for the majority of the airspace over Ireland. On reaching the Clonmel beacon, the captain speaks to the passengers once again, advising them that he is now commencing his descent into Cork Airport and should be landing within 15 minutes.

At this point, if there was congestion at the destination airport, Shannon Control would 'hold' the aircraft at Clonmel. Inbound traffic would be separated according to the runway configuration at Cork Airport and, depending on weather conditions, aircraft would be brought from the stack or holding cylinder and spaced according to prevailing conditions. Each aircraft would then make a radar-controlled approach to the instrument landing system (ILS) for the runway that is currently in use at Cork. It is always the controller's duty to ensure that the first aircraft is clear of the runway before the next one touches down. This is to ensure maximum safety in the event of the pilot having to overshoot and exercise a 'go around' procedure.

In routine circumstances, as the aircraft gets closer to its destination, Shannon Control informs the captain to contact Cork approach frequency. Eventually, when the plane is inside the final 10 miles, the flight is handed over to Cork tower frequency for the landing and arrival. At this stage the pilot is given further weather updates and extends the various flap settings. As it is a beautiful day at Cork, the captain reports that he is visual with the runway and he is cleared to land by air traffic control. Once again all checks are carried out in a uniform manner, and with a wind from the south supported by light sea breezes, the automatic pilot is disengaged, the undercarriage is lowered and a smooth landing is accomplished at Cork Airport on runway one-seven. As the plane turns off the active runway, the tower controller bids the pilots goodbye and clears them to the ground controller, who advises them at which stand the aircraft can park. As everybody works together as a unit, all these procedures fit neatly together like a giant jigsaw puzzle.

It has to be emphasised once again that nothing is left to chance and this short 30-minute domestic flight is as important to the pilots, air traffic controllers and ground personnel as any other flight that is taking place anywhere in the world.

CHAPTER SEVEN

Into the Future, Looking Back

By J. P. Crangle

WHEN CAPTAIN MIKE BANNISTER landed Concorde at Heathrow Airport, London, for the last time on 20 October 2003, he was asked by waiting reporters if this was the end of commercial supersonic flight as we know it today. His reply was very positive, indicating that he hoped it wasn't, as how could his daughter tell her children that their grandfather piloted a commercial aircraft across the Atlantic Ocean in a time space of just over three hours? The normal crossing time west to east in a subsonic aircraft such as a B747 or A330 is still more than double that of the Concorde. It's difficult to imagine that looking back just 100 years from that date, powered flight had not yet been realised.

On 17 December 1903 powered flight became a reality when two brothers, Wilbur and Orville Wright, who were nothing more than bicycle mechanics, had a dream of flight and in spite of much scepticism put that dream into action. They read and studied documents on flight as far back as the fifteenth century by great scholars of that time, such as Leonardo da Vinci and the

Montgolfier Brothers. They also examined various dissertations that were written and printed during the nineteenth century and, equipped with this knowledge, they went to the Carolinas on the east coast of the United States in 1899. In the strong winds that prevailed, they watched birds fly and particularly noted how they turned and moved in flight. They built and flew various types of gliders and then finally built the aircraft that they were going to fly. They called it simply the *Flyer*.

Not for a second did they doubt that the *Flyer* would fly, as they accepted all that their predecessors had written about the basic forces: lift, weight, thrust and drag. The only problem was that no one before had ever attempted to fly a heavier-than-air machine from the ground to a higher level strictly under its own power. Also, no one had actually steered such a craft while it was in flight. The brothers were concerned about the weight of the engine that supplied the power for the twin propellers that forced the craft forward, thus creating the necessary 'lift' on top of its wings.

At 10.35 a.m., at a place called Kill Devil Hills, Kitty Hawk, the *Flyer*'s engines were started and it moved slowly forward, with Wilbur running alongside. Gradually it rotated into the air. Orville was at the controls and he flew a sustained 120 feet across the earth's surface and was airborne for nearly 12 seconds. Not a very long distance by modern standards — only about the wingspan of a Super Boeing 747 jet — but approximately an hour later, Wilbur flew the *Flyer* again and stayed aloft for 59 seconds and covered a distance in excess of 800 feet. A new era had just begun for mankind.

Between 1903 and 1909, only very small groups of people ever witnessed the Wright brothers in flight. In 1908 Wilbur went to Europe where, outside Paris, he stayed airborne for nearly two hours. He remarked that if he had not run out of gasoline, he could have stayed up there forever. In 1909 Orville flew a demonstration for the US Army at Fort Myers and contracts were signed to manufacture a fighter plane. Later that year Wilbur flew publicly for the first time in New York to an audience of over one million people. There was definitely no turning back now. Unfortunately, in 1912 Wilbur died of typhoid aged only 45 and Orville sold out the business in 1915 for the sum of $30,000. Orville retired gracefully, having accepted many honours on his own behalf and also posthumously on behalf of his brother, and died peacefully in 1948, aged 77. It has been said many times that before the Wright brothers no one in aviation did anything fundamentally correct, and after the Wright brothers no one in aviation did anything fundamentally different. They had changed the world forever.

Between 1909 and 1929 many more heroes of aviation took to the skies, and in 1909 Louis Bleriot became the first person ever to fly across the English Channel. Glen Curtis successfully designed wing flaps and flew the first ever flying boat in 1912. In 1919 Alcock and Brown's first transatlantic non-stop flight from St John's, Newfoundland landed safely at Clifden in Co. Galway. This flight opened vast new horizons. In 1927 Charles Lindbergh, to the applause and the appreciation of millions, became the first man to fly solo across the Atlantic Ocean to France in his famous monoplane, the *Spirit of St. Louis*.

The following year the Commanding Officer of the Irish Air Corp, Commandant James Fitzmaurice, joined Captain H. Koehl and Baron von Huenefeld to enter aviation history as the first pilots to fly into the prevailing winds from east to west across the Atlantic. They took off in the Bremen from Baldonnel Aerodrome, just outside Dublin, and successfully landed at Greenly Island in Labrador. The Atlantic Ocean was at last conquered in both directions and Ireland, small as it was, played an important role in these early days of development.

The 1930s brought major changes to aviation. In 1932 Amelia Earhardt flew the Atlantic solo and Amy Johnson became the first woman to fly from England to Australia, setting a standard that very few have achieved since. Pan American Airways began to leave its mark by opening up new commercial routes from Florida to Cuba and eventually onward to South America.

Using a de Havilland Dragon Aircraft called the *Iolar* that could only accommodate five passengers, Aer Lingus Irish Airlines completed its first commercial flight from Dublin to Bristol with full passenger complement on board in May 1936. The following September it extended its services and successfully provided the first air link between Dublin and London. By 1937, Pan Am had established the first commercial flights across the Pacific, but because of the strategic importance of New York and London, the Atlantic was the real prize and Ireland was again to play a pivotal role in this connection.

Under the Ottawa International Aviation Conference of 1935 it was decided to set up a transatlantic service between the US and Great Britain using a fleet of modern flying boats, and Ireland was chosen as a major refuelling point on the direct route. The northern route was via Iceland and the southern route via the Azores. The document was signed by the various heads of state who were in attendance and it simply read as follows:

> *Subject to force majeure, all eastbound aircraft on the transatlantic air service on the direct route shall stop at the Irish Free State Airport as the first European port of call and all westbound aircraft on the direct route shall also stop at the Irish Free State Airport.*

Following two years of extensive research, Foynes on the River Shannon was selected as a flying boat terminal. .

On 11 April 1939, Foynes saw its first Boeing 314 Flying Boat touching down on the River Shannon. This graceful machine was called the *Yankee Clipper* and was under the auspices of Pan Am. It was this splendid 42-ton vessel that inaugurated the first passenger flight from the United States to Ireland on 28 June 1939 with 18 passengers on board. The eastbound route was from Long Island, New York to Botwood, Newfoundland and on to Foynes, terminating at Southampton. Because of the gathering storm in Europe, all inbound British flights arriving at Southampton returned immediately to Foynes and the relative safety of Ireland's neutrality. The journey time between Foynes and Long Island was approximately 30 hours.

This service ended in 1945 and the luxury of the flying boat was gone forever. Gone were the onboard staterooms and dining rooms, but strangely enough, the change from seaplanes to landplanes came about very quickly. Rineanna soon became known as Shannon Airport and became the major hub for all transatlantic operations on the North Atlantic. The principal route was London to New York and all aircraft flying east or west had to land at Shannon for refuelling for the 2,000-mile sector west to Gander, Newfoundland. TWA were flying piston engine Skymasters and Pan Am were flying Lockheed piston engine Constellations, or Connies as they were known, into this new transatlantic airport. Supreme comfort was offered on board BOAC piston StratoCruisers that also operated on this route. This was one of the most prestigious air routes in the world and as the Connies were pressurised to a ceiling of 18,000 feet with a ground speed of slightly over 300 m.p.h., their crossing from Shannon to Gander could be completed in less than eight hours. Their distinctive tri-rudder tail section and curved fuselage made them look very impressive when in flight.

In 1947, United States Air Force pilot Chuck Yeager broke the sound barrier at Mach 1.07 in a Bell XS-1 rocket plane. Things were now beginning to move very fast and we were definitely heading for the future.

The introduction of the jet engine totally revolutionised the airline industry and the age of the pure jet airliner dawned in 1952 when a de Havilland Comet 1, owned by BOAC, made its first scheduled flight from London to Johannesburg. In 1963, Boeing 707s were introduced on the transatlantic route and they could fly directly from New York to London, Paris or Rome.

In 1967 the Boeing 737 made its inaugural flight and became the greatest short-haul carrier of all time. It's incredible to think that somewhere in the world a Boeing 737 is either landing or taking off every five seconds. In 1969 two major milestones in aviation history occurred as the UK supersonic Concorde took to the skies, the same year Neil Armstrong walked upon the moon.

In 1970 the Boeing 747 (or the 'Jumbo', as it is affectionately known) flew commercially in Pan Am livery and entered service on the New York to London route. This aircraft has been stretched and modestly reshaped over the years to suit various configurations and at the moment the 400 series is still considered the largest passenger jet aircraft in the world, capable of carrying well over 400 passengers. Over the years, the Boeing 747 has been used by every major airline in the world and its design, without the distinctive bubble, has been developed into smaller versions, such as the Boeing 757 and the Boeing 767. Recently Airbus became its main competitor, particularly in Europe, so Boeing developed the B777, or the 'triple seven' as it is known, to rival the Airbus 330.

On 12 April 1981, exactly 20 years after Gagarin's epic space flight, the Columbia Shuttle lifted off from Cape Canaveral, returning to the earth's atmosphere without mishap and glided smoothly to land at Edwards Air Force Base. After further tests the Shuttle went fully operational in 1982.

In 2003 British Airways Concorde ceased commercial services, not because it was unsafe but because it was no longer a viable proposition. It cost more to keep it on the ground than it did in the air.

So is this the end? I think not. The Airbus consortium is to start production of its new super jet, the A380. This is an entirely new aircraft and will seat more than 550 passengers and will go into service in 2006. Let us remind ourselves that the traditional 'Jumbo' seats about 420 people, so the increase is much lower in proportion than the increase was from the B707 to the B747 back in 1970. Confirmed orders are pouring in from 66 airlines that wish to purchase this new aircraft, which will probably be configured to meet their specific needs and demands.

Boeing have decided not to press ahead with another larger plane and are quite content with the present size of its 747, but they have plans to build a near-supersonic flying wing to rival the A380. The proposed 'Sonic Cruiser' would fly just under the speed of sound, slashing about two hours off conventional transatlantic flights. Drawings of the 'Sonic Cruiser' show an aircraft quite unlike any other existing jet, with a delta wing near its tail, two smaller wings near its nose and a pair of engines blended into the wing.

In 2004, probes are on Mars sending us back pictures of the red planet that would not have been possible 20 years ago. In 1959 while I was still a young student at college I enquired if man would ever go to the moon and my physics teacher admonished me for making such an outlandish suggestion. As we know, 10 years later, man did land on the moon.

In the time span of 100 years, aviation has become a totally credible and trustworthy industry with conditions and safety standards second to none and it is openly stated that flying is the safest means of transportation ever undertaken by mankind. The amount of aircraft in the skies at any one time is breathtaking, yet research has proven that there is enough room in the heavens for a million more items of traffic if necessary. Between 1990 and 1999 statistics have confirmed that there has not been a single death attributed to an Irish or British carrier during that period.

We have arrived; this is the future.

We are at the edge of the universe.

PART TWO

The Nature of Anxiety

PHOBIAS ARE BY NO means a modern scourge. According to the results of research conducted in the United States, anxiety disorders are the primary mental health problem among American women. Men also suffer from these disorders, but not to the same extent — their major problems are alcoholism and drug abuse. Experts have described the 1970s as the decade of depression, while panic attacks, stress and anxiety-related disorders became increasingly more prevalent in the 1980s and 1990s. In the latter half of the twentieth century, between 20 to 30 million Americans per annum experienced panic attacks, phobias and other anxiety disorders. As we move forward into the twenty-first century, these problems unfortunately show no signs of diminishing.

The Difference between Fear, Anxiety and Phobias

In order to deal with your anxiety, it helps to understand its nature and to differentiate between the terms 'fear', 'anxiety' and 'phobia'. We use the word 'fear' nowadays to refer to feelings of apprehension about realistic danger: for example, your response to the appearance of a bull with a ring in its nose charging towards you down a country lane at night. This would certainly cause anybody acute anxiety. Acute fears normally subside when the cause is removed or avoided. However, the word 'fear' is also used universally to refer to conditions which involve distressing feelings. Thus it overlaps in its usage with the term 'anxiety'. Essentially, fear involves the intellectual appraisal of a threatening or dangerous situation or event; anxiety involves the emotional response or the unpleasant feelings that result when the fear is activated. The anxious individual may not know why he is afraid and the fear may be out of proportion to any realistic danger. Many authors use the terms 'free-floating' or 'general anxiety' to separate the chronic form of anxiety from the more acute form as seen in phobias.

A phobia is defined as fear that is obsessive, unrealistic and out of all proportion to any real danger in the specific object, activity or situation. Phobia sufferers recognise that their fear is unrealistic and that other people may not be unduly afraid of the same things. Because they are unable to quell their phobia it is considered irrational, although they may try to rationalise their fear. When confronted with the object or situation he or she fears, the phobic experiences a compelling desire to avoid it. Since this intense anxiety is a reaction to items or situations commonly perceived as harmless, phobias are apparently irrational, exaggerated responses.

Fear is a normal, natural, primitive response which is essential for our survival. When we perceive any event or situation to be dangerous or threatening, our bodies undergo various mental and physical changes. A message is sent from the brain to the adrenal glands which release the chemical adrenalin into the bloodstream, causing several physiological changes simultaneously. The following comments describe the trauma and fearful feelings experienced by some nervous travellers:

> 'On my last flight, when the aircraft door closed I felt a surge of heat and nausea followed by sweating palms, rapid heartbeat and an overwhelming sensation of being trapped. I wanted to scream and was afraid I would become hysterical. It took all my will-power to stay on board the plane.'

> 'I have nightmares for weeks before taking a flight. At take-off I panic and grip the seat so tightly my hands go white and numb. I feel physically ill, I can't breathe, my stomach is churning, and when we get airborne, I feel as though I have left my stomach on the ground.'

> 'Many times I sadly watched my plane take off without me and made excuses about why I missed the flight. Or else I took a cocktail of alcohol and sedatives to get myself on board. By the time the plane took off, I was in the horrors, a drunk and belligerent passenger, making a complete nuisance of myself to the cabin crew. I was a total embarrassment and eventually I stopped flying.'

Most fearful fliers, if they are being honest with themselves, can readily identify with these remarks. These symptoms are a straightforward reaction to danger or threat, whether real or imaginary, but they can terrify the victim. Apart from a fear of flying, air travellers who go through such traumas also develop a fear of the fear itself (phobophobia). Inevitably they avoid flying. When it gets to this stage they definitely need help.

Anticipatory Anxiety

'How would you like to go to New York for St Patrick's Day?' Sarah's husband asked her last January. Sarah didn't want to disappoint him and tried to mask her real feelings about her flight anxiety. She proceeded to spend the next three months living in dread of 17 March. Similar to countless others, from the moment she heard the suggestion and subsequent plans for the trip, she was constantly worried, found it difficult to function normally and could not eat or sleep properly.

There are many who can identify with Sarah and say that their life is a nightmare while they anticipate the departure date. One of the symptoms that develops is putting everything on the 'long finger' and only seeking help a week before departure. By not confronting the situation, they end up with more fear. This type of needless worrying far in advance of taking a flight is called anticipatory anxiety. You anticipate feeling uncomfortable, turbulence or becoming panic stricken. Frequently anticipatory anxiety is much worse than the experience itself. For a large number of air travellers the anxiety can start days, weeks or in some cases like Sarah, months before the flight, causing a lot of unnecessary anguish and distress. Many also find that on arrival at their destination they are unable to either enjoy their vacation or function properly at a business meeting because of the anticipatory anxiety regarding their return flight.

There are those who feel that something is wrong if they are not worrying and describe themselves as 'worriers'. When it comes to travelling by air, they say they feel in control when they worry about the forthcoming flight and therefore they are actually 'doing' something about the situation. It is as if worrying will act like a charm which will dispel the likelihood of any mishap occurring. This of course is completely useless. An example of this belief was given by Jean, a former victim who stated, 'I know it sounds crazy, but when going on a flight I genuinely believed that I should worry. When I worried I felt prepared for the worst. I wouldn't be taken by surprise if something terrible happened.' She went on to describe how she was actually enjoying a flight until she realised she wasn't worrying and felt guilty, so she decided to start worrying immediately! Worrying is a futile exercise, a total waste of energy which achieves absolutely nothing other than to entrench your fear more deeply.

Fearful fliers invariably have an arsenal of negative information and speculation about previous air mishaps. They feel the fear develops a life of its own. They can become obsessive about having all the facts concerning air disasters and feel compelled to read all the details and watch television programmes about air mishaps. When friends return from holidays or business trips, the first question they ask is, 'How was the flight? Was everything all right? Was there turbulence?' The trip itself or the holiday is of secondary interest! They also find that others seem to make a point of telling them about uncomfortable or turbulent flights they experienced themselves or that they have heard from others. All this information adds more fuel to their fear and validates their conviction that they are right to feel as they do about flying. They admit that it rarely crosses their minds that millions of people are jetting all over the world every second of the day. It is the one infrequent incident or mishap that grabs their attention and they let it feed their fear.

The Fight or Flight Response

When you are fearful of a situation where you perceive yourself to be under attack or helpless to defend yourself or when you perceive yourself to be trapped and unable to escape, a chain of biochemical changes occurs throughout your body that prepares you to cope with the threat or danger. Walter B. Cannon, an

American physiologist, was the first to describe the 'fight or flight response' in which the range of fearful feelings and emotions can fluctuate from uneasiness through agitation, dread, brooding fear and panicky feelings to sheer terror.

The first major researcher on stress, Hans Selye, was able to track precisely what happens throughout your body during the fight or flight response. The results of his findings showed that any problem, whether genuine or imagined, can cause the cerebral cortex, which is the thinking part of the brain, to alert the hypothalamus, the principal switch for the stress response situated in the mid-brain. The hypothalamus then activates the sympathetic nervous system to trigger a number of changes in your body. There is an increase in your heart rate, breathing, muscle tension, metabolism and blood pressure. Certain limbs, including your hands and feet, get cold as blood is redirected away from your extremities. Also, as blood is redirected away from the digestive system into your legs, thighs and larger muscles, you are now in a position to fight or run from your perceived source of danger. You may experience perspiration and stomach discomfort. Your pupils will dilate to intensify your vision and your hearing will become keener. As the body attempts to lighten itself in order to move faster, frequently there is a desire to pass urine or empty the bowels. Any system not required in the fight or flight response shuts down and because blood is turned away from the digestive system, this causes the feeling of stomach upset, nausea and dryness of the mouth. Every defence mechanism in your body is alerted within a fraction of a second to flee or fight the threat.

A good example of this is the case where a young boy was out playing and was knocked down by a car. The mother naturally became so stressed that she physically lifted the car off the child and pulled him out — a clear case of fight or flight. Where did she get her strength from? She accomplished this feat because her body was aroused and braced to take action.

Many find it helpful if they understand what happens throughout their body when the emergency reaction or the fight or flight response is activated. In order to better understand what is happening, we need to examine more fully the nature of anxiety with regard to the changes that take place throughout the body, the physiological dimension and also what goes on in your mind, the cognitive or mental dimension.

The Physiological Dimension

The physical sensations of fear are triggered by the brain interpreting a specific situation as dangerous or threatening. As a result, adrenalin is released into the bloodstream, which causes several physiological changes to occur simultaneously.

Some of the main physiological symptoms are:

- changes in heart rate
- muscle tension
- perspiration
- respiratory changes.

Changes in Heart Rate

When adrenalin is released into the bloodstream, the blood vessels constrict, blood pressure increases and the heart speeds up in order to pump more fuel or oxygen-laden blood around the body. This can cause palpitations which may be frightening, but this is not dangerous. The chest muscles can also become very tense, resulting in a feeling of tightness or chest pain.

Muscle Tension

The muscles require energy so that they can respond quickly. This is provided by glucose released from the liver, which reacts with the oxygen that is in the bloodstream. For this to happen, more oxygen is needed in the bloodstream, resulting in rapid breathing. Many anxious travellers are described as 'white-knuckle fliers' due to the vice-like grip they keep on the arm-rest of their seats. They invariably say that gripping gives them a feeling of security. Many find that they have pains in the muscles of their arms for hours after a flight. Other muscles that get tense are the scalp, neck and shoulders, causing headache, neck ache and in some cases a feeling of tightness around the head.

Perspiration

In preparation for action the muscles tense and subsequently heat up. Perspiration increases, thus preventing the body from overheating, in anticipation of using more energy. As perspiration increases, the mouth goes dry as the saliva glands dry up.

Respiratory Changes

Breathing is obviously the most important activity in your life. Each time you inhale air you gain oxygen and release carbon dioxide, which is a waste product. Incorrect breathing reduces the exchange of these gases, making it more difficult for you to deal with stressful events, and is a factor in anxiety and panic attacks.

Your breathing indicates the level of tension in your body. When you are tense, anxious or angry, you usually breathe in the upper chest and only the top of your lungs fill with air. At such times your breathing becomes rapid, shallow and irregular and because it occurs high in your chest, you may feel as though you are suffocating. The extra blood supplied to your muscles means that you need more oxygen, so the lungs have to work harder to inhale more air. When air is inhaled through the mouth or nose it passes down the trachea, allowing the chest to expand and the shoulders to rise. This is called thoracic breathing. When you are fearful and breathe from your chest, you may have a tendency to breathe through your mouth and to over-breathe. This can result in exhaling excess carbon dioxide in relation to the amount of oxygen in your bloodstream. As a consequence of this, a variety of symptoms can develop which include rapid heartbeat, dizziness and numb or tingling sensations in your limbs. In normal breathing the oxygen you inhale is perfectly balanced with the carbon dioxide you exhale.

Those people who have anxieties about breathing usually worry that there is insufficient air available to them. They are frequently concerned if windows and doors are closed and feel they must gasp for air. However, the problem is not the oxygen they need, but the carbon dioxide they have been breathing out excessively.

It is apparent that we can experience a variety of reactions when we become anxious. These reactions enable us to cope with situations we perceive as threatening or dangerous, whether to fight or flee from what threatens us. However, not everyone experiences all these symptoms or responses at the same time or to the same degree. In fact, most individuals have their own characteristic pattern of fear symptoms with which you can identify in the next chapter.

Threshold of Anxiety

Many individuals worry intensely that something worse will happen to them as a result of their terrifying sensations of fear. They may be relieved to learn that no matter how severe their specific symptoms of fear are, they are completely harmless. You will *not* have a heart attack, a stroke, choke or go insane. What generally happens is that as your body reaches a threshold of anxiety which it cannot sustain indefinitely, the emergency response will dissipate and your body will sooner or later return to its normal self.

Panic attacks and severe anxiety can be very frightening, but these are a straightforward and normal reaction to fear-evoking situations. If you take vigorous exercise, such as jogging, playing a game of squash or if you have a work-out in a health centre, you will experience similar sensations such as breathlessness, perspiration and increased heart rate. However, the physical feelings are not a cause of anxiety, as they are experienced in an entirely different context. It is important to understand that no matter how distressing the feelings are, they are normal, natural physical feelings and nothing that you should be alarmed about. The system that turns on your fight or flight response is the same system that turns it off. When you stop sending emergency signals to your brain that there is no emergency and that the danger has passed, all your body systems return to normal again. This is called the relaxation response.

The Cognitive or Mental Dimension

When asked what causes their fear, many reply that it is the thought of being enclosed, the take-off, the turbulence or having a panic attack. The 'thought syndrome' activates such intense feelings of fear that they would rather avoid the flight. What they fear is the sensation of fear, or phobophobia, and consequently they avoid flying. How you think always affects how you feel, and how you feel always affects how you behave. The starting point of a fear response is in your mind, your thoughts.

Fearful thoughts about flying can evoke a physical response as described and many relate how the thought of flying triggers feelings of dread, terror and a sense of doom which are so severe that they decide not to take the flight. They find that they have a pattern of thoughts about flying which seems to occur automatically whenever the prospect of flying crops up. For example, a fearful flier described how he ached to attend his only daughter's wedding in Australia, but the thought of making a 23-hour flight was too much for him. He described how the thought of flying made him break out in a cold sweat and made his heart rate increase. He sadly admitted that his fear of flying was stronger than his desire to attend his daughter's wedding. Again, the thought syndrome had won, but something can be done about this. There is help for everybody out there.

Catastrophic Thoughts

It may be of interest to those who fear the sensations of fear or of having a panic attack to learn that there is an important difference between those who have panic attacks and those who do not. Experts have found that individuals who are likely to panic have an inclination to interpret unusual or uncomfortable physical sensations in a most catastrophic manner: heart palpitations are seen as symptoms of an imminent heart attack, chest tightness and shortness of breath are viewed as evidence of suffocation, dizziness is seen as a signal that they are about to collapse. Individuals who do not panic may have similar symptoms but do not view them in the same way. Such thoughts are false and do not automatically lead to the terrifying consequences originally envisaged. It's all in the imagination.

Perception

What determines our response to any given situation or experience, no matter what it is, is our perception or interpretation of the event. An excellent example used by psychologist E. J. Bourne describes two drivers in grid-locked traffic at rush hour in a major city. One driver gets very tense, angry and frustrated as he realises that he will be home late, not only missing the start of his favourite television programme, but also missing the children before they go to bed. When he gets home he blames the traffic jam for his bad mood. The second driver is also caught up in exactly the same traffic jam but she accepts her situation. She sees this as an opportunity to relax and turns on the radio to hear the news. Instead of getting upset, she decides to listen to a new tape that she bought in order to improve her French. When she reaches her destination she is calm, relaxed and in good form. How many times have you become irate in the same situation? The simple thing to do is to divert your attention to something productive. Similarly, with flying it is not the design of the aeroplane, the engine noises or movements that arouse your fearful feelings, it is your perception of these experiences that determines your reaction and subsequent feelings. Fear is triggered from within. It is not the external events that trigger fear, it is your perception and interpretation of these sensations that determines your resulting response.

A man was flying to Los Angeles when about an hour before landing, according to his perception he felt the plane had hit something, but no explanation was forthcoming from the cockpit. He was so traumatised by this experience that he was afraid to ask the cabin crew what had happened. His perception was that the plane had bumped into something and continued flying without investigation. The plane continued on its journey and landed safely at its destination. This experience proceeded to get out of all proportion within his imagination and unfortunately he suffered panic attacks as a result of his perception. He subsequently developed a horror of flying which lasted for many years. If this gentleman had taken his courage in his hands and asked the cabin crew what had happened, he would have been given an explanation and the cabin crew would have researched the matter further. Upon subsequent investigation it was discovered that the noise he heard could have been a valve popping in one of the engine's chambers, in the same way that the valve pops on a pressure cooker and air rushes in with a bang. Each engine has a number of chambers, so there was no imminent danger regarding what he heard. He was completely reassured with the explanation and, following a short course of treatment, he is now flying again without any irrational fear. It just shows you what perception can do! If you are startled by something and you don't know what it is, always ask.

Appropriate and Inappropriate Fear Responses

Many travellers are too embarrassed to admit feeling fearful. Fear is nothing to be ashamed of. It is normal, natural, instinctive and essential for survival. Appropriate fear in response to a potentially dangerous or life-threatening situation can save your life or ensure you avoid serious injury. For example, you don't walk blindly into oncoming traffic, you don't drive around hairpin mountain bends at 60 m.p.h. and you make sure all the gas jets on the kitchen cooker are safely switched off when you have finished cooking. You take precautions to ensure your personal safety. On the other hand, a fear response to a situation that does not warrant any fear is inappropriate and can cause unnecessary anguish and distress. For example, those who perceive spiders, bridges, tunnels or flying in aeroplanes to be life threatening or dangerous generally experience fear that is excessive and out of proportion to any real danger in these situations. They would prefer to avoid the source of their fear, but unfortunately such evasion can place severe limitations on their ambitions and can seriously disrupt their lifestyle. When you avoid the source of your fear, such as refusing to take a flight, you are only getting temporary relief from the anxiety. By avoiding the flight you only strengthen the fear.

There is a difference between an appropriate fear response to a possible threatening or dangerous event and an inappropriate fear response to a harmless event. Imagine that it is 2 a.m. The house has been locked and secured, the family are all home and asleep in bed. Suddenly you are awakened by the sound of glass breaking and you hear an intruder stealthily moving around the house downstairs. Instantly you are wide awake and your brain triggers the alarm signal to activate the emergency fight or flight response. Your heart pounds, you feel breathless, you perspire, your muscles tense, your senses are sharpened, your hearing becomes more acute and the pupils of your eyes dilate to enable you to see more clearly. What you experience is a normal, natural response to a possible life-threatening situation. You perceive danger and react accordingly. You do not know if the intruder is armed with a knife or a gun. Your body is braced to take some course of action — either waken your loved ones and run to safety or security (this is the flight response) or take a golf club or poker and go downstairs and tackle the intruder (this is the fight response). You must do something, as it is highly unlikely that you will go back to sleep!

When the situation has been successfully resolved, when the burglar has been apprehended and the police have taken him away, your major focus is the immediate situation. You will probably ask yourself questions. Why didn't the security alarm go off? How did he get into the house? What damage has been done? Has anything been stolen? Is the house insurance adequate to cover everything? Your feeling of fear has become secondary in importance. What you have experienced was an appropriate response to a real-life, potentially dangerous situation. Your perception was that your life and that of your family was in danger and you responded appropriately.

Fear and even terror in response to harmless creatures such as spiders, kittens, plants, balloons, bridges, aeroplanes, the darkness of night and certain colours such as purple is quite common. An inappropriate fear response to a harmless, non-threatening creature such as a house spider can be illustrated by a man sitting quietly, reading a magazine. If he happens to see a spider weaving its web, he can experience anxiety symptoms similar to those experienced in response to a burglar breaking into his house at night. However, when the spider has been taken away, his major focus is on his fear: 'I'm so frightened, I can't get my breath. I'm shaking. I hate spiders.' His primary focus is on his distress and feelings of fear, whereas the spider is a secondary consideration. Do you see how the focus reverses?

It is interesting to note that while some people have sympathy for such sufferers, many others, who do not suffer similar anxieties, have little or no sympathy for them. For example, it is possible that those with a severe fear of flying admit that they have no comprehension as to how their friends could possibly fear water, bees or eating in restaurants, yet they can have total sympathy and readily identify with other aerophobics. A former victim admitted that she had no sympathy for her daughter who had a fear of spiders, yet she admired the fact that her daughter had no fear of flying!

CHAPTER NINE

Conquer Your Fear of Flying

Your Personal Flight Anxiety Profile

'WHEN I WAS YOUNGER I always thought this fear of flying would go away some day. I used to think that when I'm older I'll probably grow out of it. If anything, it's got worse.' This is a remark frequently heard from older people who on approaching middle age realise that they have spent a considerable number of years avoiding holidays abroad or make business trips overland rather than take a flight. For so many years they have let their fear dictate their decision not to fly. When you avoid taking a flight you are relieved of your immediate anxiety, but in fact you are only strengthening the fear, and the longer you avoid getting help for this problem, the worse it becomes. The fear just gets stronger and deeper. However, the good news is that fear of flying is a reversible problem and responds remarkably well to proper treatment.

The first step towards conquering your fear of flying is to admit you have a problem. The second step is your determination to take positive action to deal with the problem, because it is highly unlikely that one day you will wake up to discover that your fear of flying has gone away. The third step takes a lot of personal courage and involves confronting the fear and learning how to deal with it. Taking alcohol or tranquillisers is not the cure; burying your head in the sand achieves nothing. The next chapter will deal with techniques to help you conquer your fear of flying. In order to deal with your fear efficiently and to benefit from the instructions, it is necessary to first identify your individual pattern of fear. The following surveys will help you assess:

- the magnitude of your flight anxiety
- your pattern of fear symptoms
- the flight-related situations that trigger your fear
- the anxiety-evoking situations that are linked to your fear.

It is now recommended that you complete the following questionnaires to establish the extent or intensity of your fear at this point and again on the completion of the self-management programme, which will be outlined in the next chapter.

Anxiety Scale

The following anxiety scale is a quick, simple method of evaluating the degree of anxiety you experience in response to any threatening situation, including flying. It is marked from zero, which indicates complete calm, with ratings signifying increasing levels of anxiety to 10, which represents sheer terror or panic. Simply mark on the scale the degree of fear you experience at the prospect of taking a flight.

0 1	2 3	4 5	6 7	8 9	10
Calm	Relaxed	Average anxiety	Very anxious	Terror	Panic

Flight Stress Symptoms Checklist

Whenever you become fearful or anxious, you experience a pattern of fear responses. Please examine the following checklist of symptoms and indicate how you react, or think you would react if you have never flown, at the prospect of taking a flight. Mark each item on the scale as it applies to you on the following zero to three scale, then add all your scores to find your total flight stress symptoms score.

0 = Never
1 = Occasionally
2 = Frequently
3 = Always

(a) Central Nervous System

State of mind

1. I can't concentrate	0	1	2	3
2. I become absent-minded	0	1	2	3
3. I fear I can't sleep	0	1	2	3
4. I have nightmares	0	1	2	3
5. I fear I'm going to die	0	1	2	3
6. I get confused	0	1	2	3
7. I'll lose control	0	1	2	3
8. I'll become hysterical	0	1	2	3
9. I feel hypercritical	0	1	2	3
10. I feel hypervigilant	0	1	2	3
11. I fear I'll go insane	0	1	2	3
12. I have feelings of unreality	0	1	2	3
13. I'll have a stroke	0	1	2	3
14. I'll have a heart attack	0	1	2	3

→

State of mind (*cont'd*)

15. I'll scream	0	1	2	3
16. I'll make a fool of myself	0	1	2	3
17. I'm scared	0	1	2	3
18. I'm worried	0	1	2	3
19. I feel bad-tempered	0	1	2	3
20. I feel vulnerable	0	1	2	3
21. I have irrational thoughts	0	1	2	3
Score =				

(b) Bodily Symptoms

These will be categorised according to the relevant physiological system.

Cardiovascular system

1. Palpitations	0	1	2	3
2. Irregular heartbeat	0	1	2	3
3. Chest pains	0	1	2	3
4. Dizziness	0	1	2	3
5. Increased blood pressure	0	1	2	3
6. Faintness	0	1	2	3
Score =				

Respiratory system

1. Rapid breathing	0	1	2	3
2. Hyperventilation	0	1	2	3
3. Shallow breathing	0	1	2	3

→

Respiratory system (*cont'd*)

4. Irregular breathing	0	1	2	3
5. Unable to take deep breath	0	1	2	3
6. Choking sensation	0	1	2	3
7. Lump in throat	0	1	2	3

Score =

Muscle tension

1. Clench my jaw	0	1	2	3
2. Tremble	0	1	2	3
3. Weakness	0	1	2	3
4. Fidget constantly	0	1	2	3
5. Tension headache	0	1	2	3
6. Clench my hands	0	1	2	3
7. Feel unco-ordinated	0	1	2	3
8. Difficulty speaking coherently	0	1	2	3
9. Hyperactive	0	1	2	3

Score =

Gastrointestinal symptoms

1. Nausea	0	1	2	3
2. Vomiting	0	1	2	3
3. Diarrhoea	0	1	2	3
4. Mouth dryness	0	1	2	3
5. Loss of appetite	0	1	2	3

Score =

Other symptoms

1. Toilet frequency	0	1	2	3
2. Blurred vision	0	1	2	3
3. Acute hearing re: engine sounds	0	1	2	3
4. Face flushes	0	1	2	3
5. Face pales	0	1	2	3
6. Perspiration	0	1	2	3
7. Hands/feet feel cold	0	1	2	3
8. Tingling sensations	0	1	2	3
9. Numbing sensations	0	1	2	3

Score =

Add all your scores to obtain the total score for your flight stress symptoms checklist.

Total Score =

Questionnaire Form re: Fear of Flying

The following questionnaire lists various situations that are part of the flying experience. To indicate the extent of your anxiety in each situation, circle the number which most appropriately describes how anxious each situation makes you feel. You should then add all your scores to obtain your total fear of flying score.

The following situations make me feel:	No anxiety	Little anxiety	Moderate anxiety	Extreme anxiety	Panic
1. Looking through travel brochures	0	1	2	3	4
2. Purchasing flight tickets	0	1	2	3	4
3. Packing/preparing for a flight	0	1	2	3	4
4. Saying goodbye to family	0	1	2	3	4
5. Saying goodbye to friends	0	1	2	3	4
6. Driving to the airport	0	1	2	3	4
7. Walking into departures	0	1	2	3	4
8. Waiting at check-in desk	0	1	2	3	4
9. Watching removal of my luggage	0	1	2	3	4
10. Going through security	0	1	2	3	4
11. Waiting at boarding gate	0	1	2	3	4
12. Flying to a foreign country	0	1	2	3	4
13. Flying with family members	0	1	2	3	4
14. Hearing flight call	0	1	2	3	4
15. Flying alone	0	1	2	3	4
16. Walking towards plane	0	1	2	3	4
17. Boarding plane	0	1	2	3	4
18. Losing self-control in public	0	1	2	3	4
19. Taking flight by day	0	1	2	3	4
20. Prospect of aircraft crashing	0	1	2	3	4
21. Sitting next to window	0	1	2	3	4
22. Captain's announcements	0	1	2	3	4
23. Engine noises at take-off	0	1	2	3	4
24. Flying in stormy weather	0	1	2	3	4
25. Safety demonstration	0	1	2	3	4
26. Cabin crew's announcement	0	1	2	3	4

→

The following situations make me feel:	No anxiety	Little anxiety	Moderate anxiety	Extreme anxiety	Panic
27. Sitting in centre seat	0	1	2	3	4
28. Sound of door closing	0	1	2	3	4
29. 'Fasten seat belt' illuminating	0	1	2	3	4
30. Awareness of cabin pressurisation	0	1	2	3	4
31. Watching cabin crew check seatbelts	0	1	2	3	4
32. Flying with friends	0	1	2	3	4
33. Lurch backwards as plane moves to runway	0	1	2	3	4
34. Plane taxiing to runway	0	1	2	3	4
35. Having no control in the situation	0	1	2	3	4
36. Flying at night	0	1	2	3	4
37. Being thrust back at acceleration	0	1	2	3	4
38. Roar of engines at lift-off	0	1	2	3	4
39. Taking off into the air	0	1	2	3	4
40. Sound: undercarriage retracting	0	1	2	3	4
41. Chimes: cabin crew call bell	0	1	2	3	4
42. Seeing cabin crew enter/exit cockpit	0	1	2	3	4
43. Walking around cabin	0	1	2	3	4
44. Flying over water	0	1	2	3	4
45. Plane turning in flight	0	1	2	3	4
46. Walking to the toilet	0	1	2	3	4
47. Sitting in aisle seat	0	1	2	3	4
48. Flying over mountains	0	1	2	3	4
49. Flying in calm weather	0	1	2	3	4

$\longrightarrow$

The following situations make me feel:	No anxiety	Little anxiety	Moderate anxiety	Extreme anxiety	Panic
50. Looking out window	0	1	2	3	4
51. Announcement: fasten seatbelts — turbulence expected	0	1	2	3	4
52. Unfamiliar engine noises	0	1	2	3	4
53. Awareness of flying at 30,000 feet	0	1	2	3	4
54. Unexpected turbulence	0	1	2	3	4
55. Preparation for landing	0	1	2	3	4
56. Instruction: fasten seatbelts descending	0	1	2	3	4
57. Descending closer to runway	0	1	2	3	4
58. Roar of engines at touchdown	0	1	2	3	4
Total fear of flying score =					

Fear Survey

There are many anxious air travellers who also experience severe anxiety or distress in situations apart from flying. In 1973, Joseph Wolpe, an American psychiatrist, developed the Fear Survey Schedule. The following is an amended version of this survey. To establish the degree of fear these situations cause, simply rate your fearfulness in response to each item:

0 = No anxiety

1 = Little anxiety

2 = Average anxiety

3 = Very anxious

4 = Extreme anxiety

1. Falling	0	1	2	3	4
2. High places on land	0	1	2	3	4
3. Physical injury	0	1	2	3	4
4. Dying	0	1	2	3	4
5. Elevators	0	1	2	3	4
6. Tunnels	0	1	2	3	4
7. Subways	0	1	2	3	4
8. Thunder	0	1	2	3	4
9. Lightning	0	1	2	3	4
10. Wind	0	1	2	3	4
11. Dull weather	0	1	2	3	4
12. Crowds	0	1	2	3	4
13. Looking foolish	0	1	2	3	4
14. Large open spaces	0	1	2	3	4
15. Enclosed spaces	0	1	2	3	4
16. Sight of deep water	0	1	2	3	4
17. Darkness	0	1	2	3	4
18. Strange places	0	1	2	3	4
19. Being alone	0	1	2	3	4
20. People in authority	0	1	2	3	4
21. Train journeys	0	1	2	3	4
22. Bus journeys	0	1	2	3	4
23. Car journeys	0	1	2	3	4
24. Boat journeys	0	1	2	3	4
25. Aeroplane journeys	0	1	2	3	4

Score =

There are many who have no fear of flying yet still avoid air travel due to an acute fear of heights or enclosed spaces. In some cases it may be necessary to seek help in order to address these fears first.

Overall Total

Now that you have completed your flight anxiety profile, fill in your total scores in the following table. Following this, complete the forms again after you have finished the self-management programme and you will find it a worthwhile exercise to compare the changes in your scores. You can do this for all subsequent flights and monitor your improvement accordingly.

Flight anxiety profile	Total scores		
	Before programme	After programme	After flight
1. Anxiety scale 2. Flight stress symptoms 3. Fear of flying survey 4. Fear survey			

Self-management Programme

WHEN YOU HAVE COMPLETED the flight anxiety profile you will have a greater awareness of the depth of your fear, the associated flight-related situations that trigger it and the anxiety symptoms that you subsequently experience. It is important to remember that fear of flying is not a disease or infection or beyond your control. People are not born with such fears: they acquire or learn them in the same way other things are learned. Remember, the longer the problem is left unaddressed, the more entrenched it becomes. However, it is reversible and responds remarkably well to intervention. The tragedy lies not in having a fear of flying, but rather in not availing of help to conquer it. In order to overcome the problem, it is vital to understand that it is possible to learn how to conquer your fear of flying, provided you have the following essential ingredients.

Requirements for Your Self-management Programme

Personal Responsibility

It is futile to chastise or criticise yourself for having a fear of flying. Accept that you have a problem, but now you must take responsibility for what you are going to do about it. Remember, there is a big difference between saying 'flying terrifies me' and 'I'm terrified when I fly' or 'lifts scare me' and 'I'm scared when I'm in a lift.' The fear is not in the lift or inside the aeroplane; the fear originates within yourself. We all have fears — in fact, we own them. Nobody can take away someone else's fear. The one and only person who can conquer your fear is you.

Ultimately you are the one responsible for holding onto your fear or for doing something about it. Nothing changes without your consent. When you accept this responsibility and make a decision to do something about it, you are empowering yourself to take control. You are the one who keeps the fear alive; you are also the one with the power to deal with it. You will be as successful at overcoming your fear of flying as you genuinely determine you want to be. Before embarking on the self-management programme, it is essential to have the following qualities to be successful. These are not daunting and are simple, straightforward guidelines that will help you.

Determination

There is a big difference between the desire and the determination to achieve a personal goal, whether it is with regard to over-coming an addiction, an unhealthy habit, a phobia or pursuing a course of study. There are many examples of smokers who say, 'Some day I'll quit, maybe after Christmas', overweight people who say, 'I would love to lose weight. Some day I'll go on a strict diet. In the meantime pass me a large slice of that delicious Pavlova' or fearful air travellers who reflect on the numerous opportunities they have let slip and continue to delay seeking help: 'When the children are back at school' or 'I'll wait till summer' or 'When my husband retires.'

Motivation

Your ability to do something about your problem depends on your motivation — and motivation is the key to change. Ask yourself if you are genuinely motivated to confront your problem and learn to use new patterns of thought and behaviour. If you are experiencing considerable inconvenience, missing out on career opportunities and promotion, bonus flights or overseas holiday travel because of genuine distress at the prospect of taking a flight, you are likely to be highly motivated to do something about a problem that is seriously restricting your lifestyle. Many see their fear as a personal challenge and eventually realise they are tired of fear dictating their choices in life or standing in the way of their dreams and ambitions.

The Following Obstacles Should be Avoided

There are certain factors that can undermine your motivation. Whereas you consciously want to overcome your fear of flying, your motivation may not be strong enough to surmount the anxiety generated by your fear. This is regarded as a 'pay-off'. Many years ago Sigmund Freud referred to the notion of unconscious pay-offs as 'secondary gains'. Whenever there is a strong mental opposition to overcoming any prolonged condition such as depression, alcoholism, drug addictions or obesity, secondary gains are frequently active. If you have a problem developing or maintaining the motivation to do something about your situation, simply ask yourself what rewards or pay-offs you are getting for staying the way you are. Examples of pay-offs or secondary gains for not overcoming the fear of flying include the following.

- Many fearful air travellers admit to secretly enjoying a certain notoriety when the topic of air travel comes up in conversation. They enjoy being the centre of attention their fear of air transport generates among friends. They actually enjoy dramatising their sensational reactions to flying, much to the amusement and entertainment of friends and colleagues.

- Countless others have a deep-rooted belief that overcoming their fear of flying is too much hard work. They believe they are not strong enough to confront their fear and learn to conquer it.

- Others find they enjoy the extra sympathy and attention they gain from loved ones when the prospect of taking a flight arises.

- In some cases the fear of flying can be a form of self-protection, an acceptable excuse for not visiting people you are not comfortable with who live overseas.

Secondary gains as an impediment to motivation and conquering the fear of flying occur in a small percentage of fearful fliers. If you feel you are having difficulties with motivation, it is important to ask yourself if you are getting a pay-off for not learning how to overcome your problem.

Commitment

For many, the fear of flying has been endured for years. It would therefore be unrealistic to think that you can recover from this problem overnight. When you make the decision to do something about your fear, your initial enthusiasm will certainly get you started on your recovery programme. However, it is not always easy to maintain that high level of enthusiasm unless you have a genuine commitment to persevere with the exercises and instructions involved in your self-management programme. There will be times when your motivation will tend to fluctuate, but making a determined commitment to continue will make a real difference between a partial or a full reversal of your fear of flying. You do not fail until you stop trying.

Willingness to Change

It is important to remember that change will not take place without your consent. It is impossible for change to occur unless you really want it to, and you must experiment with new modes of thought, feelings and behaviour. You may find it difficult to believe that you could ever feel remotely comfortable at the prospect of taking a flight, but it will happen. It requires courage to learn how to take control of your fear and confront the situation, which you will learn to do gradually. It will mean giving up some pay-offs. It also means learning simple skills which are highly effective in reducing your fear, which are outlined in the following section.

Ideal Image

Before commencing the self-management programme, take a few moments to answer the following questions, which should help you clarify what you wish to conquer.

1. What am I missing by staying as I am?
2. What are the advantages of air travel?
3. What differences would overcoming my fear of flying make to me personally, my career, family and relationships?
4. What would the positive results be on my life?
5. What friends or family living overseas would I most like to visit?
6. What countries would I like to visit?
7. What is my ideal self-image when travelling by air?

Many sufferers find they are the butt of amusement among their well-meaning friends or relatives who dismiss their fear of flying with remarks such as 'Don't be silly, there's nothing to be afraid of, 'Just pull yourself together, get a grip on yourself' or 'Take a few drinks and you'll be fine.' Unfortunately, overcoming fear is not that easy. Such advice is not the answer to the problem and is rarely helpful. You will never improve your game of tennis, your cooking or your attempts at learning to play the guitar if others frequently trivialise your efforts or undermine your confidence. In addition to having the right frame of mind, being receptive to the skills you are now going to learn will help you progress and achieve your objective.

Anti-anxiety Antidote

Some of the factors that contribute to your fear of flying have already been discussed with regard to mistaken beliefs about unfamiliar engine noises, turbulence and other matters. What now remains is how to deal with the mental and physical symptoms of your fear. The following section describes how you can develop techniques that will enable you to take control of your anxiety. This includes instruction in:

1. **Relaxation,** which includes breathing techniques and progressive muscle relaxation. This will enable you to counteract the physical effects of anxiety. Instruction in pleasant mental relaxation by visualisation is also outlined.
2. **Thought control,** which is very important in learning how to cope with the negative thoughts you associate with air travel. Instruction on negative thought blocking and positive thought control is also outlined.

When you have achieved control of your thoughts and behaviour, you will have a different attitude towards flying. Then you will be ready to follow the step-by-step instructions on how to confront your fear of flying.

Relaxation

Deep relaxation is much more than unwinding at the end of the day by having a cup of coffee and watching something on television. This may be a pleasant and basic form of relaxation in which most people indulge, but there is another more effective form, which is the regular practice of deep relaxation, described below.

The natural remedy for anxiety is relaxation. It is a well-known fact that deep relaxation refers to a specific physiological state that is the exact opposite to the way your body reacts when confronting a fear-evoking situation. This state was described by Herbert Benson in 1975 and is called the 'relaxation response', explained and referred to previously. The ability to develop deep relaxation is the foundation of this programme, which is designed to conquer the fear of flying.

Learning to relax is like learning any other new skill. It requires motivation, perseverance, an understanding of the basic principles involved and regular practice. It is suggested that you make a commitment to practise relaxation daily. Ideally you should set aside 20 minutes each day. For maximum effectiveness you should do this exercise twice daily. You will find the practice routine very pleasant and after two or three weeks you will definitely feel more relaxed. Much is written regarding the additional benefits of relaxation, which include a reduction in insomnia, headaches, improvement in memory and concentration and a considerable increase in energy.

Breathing

Breathing is essential to life. Every organ in your body needs oxygen to stay alive. The body needs a continuous supply of oxygen as well as a method of releasing waste carbon dioxide. This is the task of the blood circulation and lungs, where the exchange of gases occurs. Poor breathing habits reduce the flow of these gases, making it more difficult for you to deal with stressful events. Incorrect breathing patterns contribute to panic attacks, muscle tension, headaches and fatigue and can lead to hyperventilation.

Hyperventilation

We inhale oxygen from the air and we exhale carbon dioxide, which is a waste gas, but if we breathe out too much carbon dioxide we hyperventilate and become more excitable, nervous and jittery. The reduction of carbon dioxide in the blood can cause your heart to pump faster and harder in addition to making lights seem brighter and sounds louder. If the blood vessels in your brain constrict (tighten), it is more difficult for the blood to transport the oxygen and this can result in dizziness, disorientation and a lack of concentration. The feelings are surreal and everything seems to be happening at a distance.

The conventional method for dealing with hyperventilation is to breathe into a paper bag. In this way you are rebreathing your carbon dioxide back into your body. Another technique is to cup your hands together over your mouth and nose and breathe calmly and slowly. This procedure is also very effective and restores the normal balance of oxygen to the carbon dioxide in your bloodstream.

It is important to stress that you cannot relax if you are not breathing properly and it is advisable to develop abdominal breathing in order to increase your lung capacity to breathe more deeply. This will help you slow down your breathing, which in turn redresses the balance of oxygen and carbon dioxide.

Abdominal or Diaphragmatic Breathing

When you inhale, air is drawn deep into your lungs and exhaled as the diaphragm contracts and expands. Your diaphragm is a sheet-like muscle that separates the lungs from the abdomen. It assists your breathing by expanding and contracting as you inhale and exhale. When you are relaxed you breathe deeply from your abdomen. This pattern of breathing is a very simple and effective method of relaxation and is essential for your health and for anxiety management. In addition to boosting your oxygen exchange and excreting bodily toxins through the lungs, your heart rate and blood pressure is lowered. Deep breathing also helps to distract you from stressful situations and increases your sense of control. It is extremely difficult to feel tense or anxious and to breathe from your abdomen at the same time.

A few minutes of abdominal breathing is the simplest way to trigger a relaxation response. If you can control your breathing, you can control your heart rate and most other symptoms of anxiety. Diaphragmatic or abdominal breathing can also effectively reduce the symptoms of hyperventilation within a very short space of time. Among the many benefits the following are a few rewards of deep breathing.

- There is a greater supply of oxygen to the brain, which controls the body.
- It is a proven fact that your concentration will improve.
- You will feel calmer and relaxed.

But first, before going through the abdominal breathing exercises, it is suggested that you check your breathing pattern by going through the following steps. Close your eyes, place one hand on your chest and the other on your abdomen just below your waist. Continue breathing normally and notice how you are breathing and which hand rises most as you inhale. If the hand on your chest rises more, you are breathing from the chest or thorax. If it is the hand on your stomach that rises more, you are breathing from the abdomen or diaphragm. To enable you to switch from chest to abdominal breathing, first breathe out fully, exhaling all the air from the lower part of your lungs. You will find it easier and natural to draw in a deep diaphragmatic breath on your next inhalation. There are many ways to practise abdominal or diaphragmatic breathing, either standing, sitting or walking. However, while you are learning, it is easier to practise lying down, as the following illustrations and instruction will demonstrate.

Abdominal Breathing Exercises

1. Lie down on a rug or blanket. Place pillows or cushions behind your head, neck, spinal column and the small of your back. Stretch your legs and keep them slightly apart.

2. Scan your body for any tension and loosen it. To avoid visual distractions, you may wish to close your eyes or focus your gaze on a particular spot on the ceiling. As you go through the exercises, take your time and proceed at your own pace.
3. Gently place one hand on your chest and the other on your stomach.
4. Inhale slowly and deeply through your nose, mentally say the word 'calm' and as you slowly exhale through your mouth, repeat the word 'relax'. Your stomch will rise and your chest will move slightly.
5. Continue inhaling through your nose or mouth slowly and deeply and try to take twice as long to exhale through your

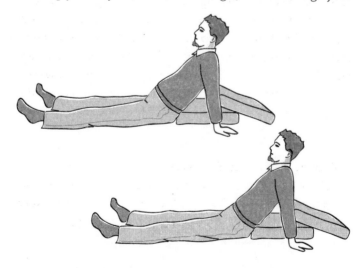

mouth, making a gentle 'phewww' sound as though you are blowing bubbles.

6. Focus on the sound and pleasant experience of deep breathing as you become more and more relaxed.

7. When you are confident that you have achieved diaphragmatic breathing on your back, bring your body up to a 45° angle with your hands supporting you from behind. Continue diaphragmatic breathing until you feel you can comfortably breathe from the diaphragm in this position.

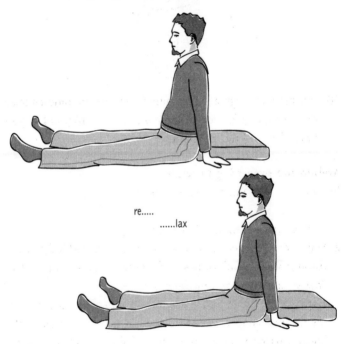

re.....
......lax

8. Now raise your body up to a 90° sitting angle and continue deep breathing.

9. Finally, stand with your hands behind the back of your neck and carry on breathing from the diaphragm.

10. Practise diaphragmatic breathing for five to ten minutes once or twice a day for one to three weeks or until you feel you have mastered the technique.

Abdominal Breathing Practice
In order to achieve maximum effectiveness:

1. Train yourself to inhale slowly and deeply.
2. Pause for a few seconds, then exhale slowly and fully, either through your mouth or nose, whichever is more comfortable.
3. Always take twice as long to exhale.
4. Focus on your abdomen extending and retracting as you inhale and exhale air in and out of your lungs and enjoy the lovely sensation of relaxation that follows. If at all possible try to exhale through your mouth. You may find it helpful to silently repeat the word 'calm', 'relax', 'loosen up' or any other relaxing word as you breathe out.

The following exercises can be used to develop abdominal breathing and release mild tension or severe anxiety.

1. Loosen belts or neckties and make sure you are sitting in a comfortable chair. Place your arms on the arm-rests of the chair, legs uncrossed, feet apart and placed flat on the floor.
2. Check your body for any tension, loosen up completely, unwind and let go.
3. Mentally try to put aside any stressful thoughts or problems.
4. Start by inhaling slowly and deeply into your abdomen.
5. Pause for a moment, then exhale slowly through your mouth or nose.
6. Repeat this cycle twice more, each time inhaling deeply and exhaling fully.
7. Continue to inhale slowly through your nose, pause and hold your breath for a count of three.
8. Exhale slowly through your mouth or nose for a count of five or six or for as long as it takes. Always try to take twice as long to exhale.
9. Repeat this cycle twice.
10. Inhale slowly through your nose, pause and count to five.
11. Exhale slowly through your mouth or nose for a count of 10 if possible or for as long as it takes.
12. Repeat this cycle twice more.

If possible schedule a regular time to practise abdominal breathing each day in order to develop the habit of deep breathing. When you have learned how to breathe deeply, you will find you can apply the exercises in any situation that causes you to feel tense or anxious, whether sitting or standing. With regular practice you will achieve a state of relaxation within approximately three minutes of breathing from the abdomen.

Progressive Muscle Relaxation

Relaxation is very important when learning to take control of anxiety. When you know how to relax your body, you will automatically reduce the unpleasant symptoms of fear. Learning how to remain calm in the face of fear can give you a great feeling of self-control.

In 1929, a Chicago physician named Dr Edmund Jacobson published a book on progressive relaxation. His technique is based on the rationale that the body responds to anxiety-provoking thoughts, events and situations with muscle tension. The result of this physiological tension adds to the individual's feelings of anxiety. Deep muscle relaxation decreases muscle tension and is not compatible with anxiety. The regular practice of progressive muscle relaxation enables you to control your anxiety and panic attacks, confront your fears and enjoy a general improvement in well-being.

Progressive Muscle Relaxation Techniques

The regular practice of progressive muscle relaxation includes:

- decrease in heart rate
- breathing slows down
- decrease in blood pressure
- muscles relax
- reduction in anxious thoughts
- reduction in general anxiety
- greater control of panic attacks.

Additional benefits include improved concentration and sleep patterns, an increase in self-esteem and, as already noted, a general improvement in well-being.

Basic Preparation

Before embarking on any form of relaxation it is advisable to go through the following preparation routine.

1. The relaxation exercises can be practised either lying down or sitting in a chair. Always ensure that your head, neck and back are supported and find a quiet place where you are unlikely to be disturbed.
2. Loosen any tight clothes and sit back comfortably in the chair.
3. Close your eyes and mentally set aside any worries, problems or concerns. Let yourself drift into a pleasant, neutral state of mind.
4. Scan your body for tension. Try to loosen up, unwind and let go.
5. Don't try to force the relaxation or worry whether you are doing it properly, just loosen up and let yourself go.
6. If you have an injury or a weak muscle group, it is advisable to use great caution when tensing that particular muscle group. Perhaps it is better to skip it completely.
7. Start by taking a few deep abdominal breaths, exhaling very slowly. Each time you exhale, visualise the tension evaporating and drifting away.
8. When you tense a muscle group, hold the tension for approximately 10 seconds, focus on the build-up of tension, then release the tension quickly and concentrate on the contrast between tension and relaxation. Enjoy the pleasant feeling of relaxation flowing into the muscle group for about 15 seconds.
9. While working on a specific muscle group, try to keep the other muscles relaxed.
10. As you proceed through the relaxation routine of tensing and relaxing your muscles, try to apply the same timespans of tensing for 10 seconds and relaxing for 15 seconds.
11. It is helpful to mentally say to yourself, 'relax, loosen up, let go' as you release the tension and relax completely.
12. You only need to tense and relax each muscle group once, but if certain muscles are particularly tense, repeat the exercise for two or three more cycles.

Progressive Muscle Relaxation Procedures

The following instructions are outlined to include the four major muscle groups, which are as follows.

Hands and forearms

- Start by clenching your fists tightly, pause and hold that tension for approximately 10 seconds, focus on the tension, then relax for almost 15 seconds and focus on the feelings of looseness in your hands in contrast to the tension.
- Continue to tighten your forearms, elbows and biceps, bend them up towards your shoulders, pause, concentrate on the tension, then straighten out your arms and relax.

Remember to focus on the contrast between the tension and lovely feelings of relaxation.

Head, face, neck and shoulders

- Concentrate on the muscles in your head. Wrinkle your forehead, raise your eyebrows as high as you can, pause, feel the tension, then relax your eyebrows, smoothe the furrows across your forehead and relax.
- Continue to tense the muscles in your face. Keep your eyes closed, squint your eyes and eyelids and tighten the muscles around your eyes, pause, feel the tautness, now relax and let the tension melt away.
- Clench your jaw tightly, pause and relax.
- Now pucker your lips, pause and relax. Let your lips part slightly and your jaw hang loose and slack as you relax the muscles around your mouth.
- Tense the muscles throughout your neck by drawing back your neck as far as is comfortable. Now tighten these muscles, pause and relax. Gently let your neck fall forward

127

onto your chest and feel the tension in the back of your neck. Now slowly straighten your head and rotate your head to the left and right, pause, feel the tension, then bring your head back to a comfortable position and enjoy the relaxation flowing throughout your neck and head.

- Shrug your shoulders and raise them up to your ears, pause, feel the tension, now loosen up and let your shoulders drop down and relax. Enjoy the feelings of relaxation flowing throughout your shoulders. Continue to tighten your shoulder blades, draw them back as far as is comfortable, pause, notice the tension, let go and relax. Feel the tension evaporating and savour the pleasant sensation of relaxation.

Chest, stomach and lower back

- Concentrate on your chest, inhale, fill your lungs with air, pause, hold your breath, feel the tension, now slowly exhale the tension and feel your chest becoming loose and slack. Continue breathing normally.
- Tense your stomach muscles by pulling in your stomach, pause, feel the tautness, now unravel that tension, let go and relax.
- Tense your lower back by arching it without straining, pause, note the tension and relax. If you suffer lower back pain, it is advisable to skip this exercise.
- Spend a few moments savouring the feelings of relaxation flowing through these muscles and observe how feelings of relaxation always follow the release of tension.

Thighs, legs and feet

- Continue to tense the muscles all along your thighs, pause, hold the tension and relax. Note the contrast between tension and relaxation. Tighten your calf muscles by curling your toes downwards, feel the tension in your shins, pause and relax. Now curl your toes upwards towards you, note the tension in your calves, pause and relax.

Spend a few moments checking your body for any remaining areas of tension and repeat two or three tense/relax exercises. Relish the pleasant sensations of relaxation spreading throughout your body, starting from your head and flowing into all your muscles. Focus on the calm, peaceful feelings of blissful relaxation. The progressive muscle relaxation routine will take 20–30 minutes of practice in the early stages. It is important to practise regularly and it is suggested you set aside a certain time each day to do this. When you master the skills, you will find you can achieve relaxation within 10–15 minutes. Many find they learn to relax faster by listening to relaxation exercises on an audio cassette. You might like to purchase a professionally recorded tape on progressive relaxation.

Visualisation

When you have worked through the progressive muscle relaxation procedures, it is also helpful to spend a few minutes relaxing mentally. This will further enhance your overall sense of relaxation. Visualisation involves imagining a relaxing scene where you feel safe, secure and very calm. It can be a memory of a special occasion, it can be indoors or outdoors or you can create your own special haven. The main objective of visualisation is to use your imagination to create a special relaxing scene which, with practice, will become entrenched in your mind and which you can retrieve within a few seconds when you wish to calm yourself and switch off fearful thoughts.

Have you ever been some place where you felt very peaceful and all your worries and problems dissolved and melted away? Maybe it was the sight of a beautiful sunset, a favourite beach, swans on a river, a special room in your parents' house or your own home. Was there a family occasion with loved ones when you felt carefree and happy or a special childhood memory you cherish? It doesn't matter where or what your special scene is, as long as you associate it with peace, harmony and security. When you have decided where your special scene is, it is important to visualise it clearly so that it totally absorbs your attention. The more vividly you create the scene, the more life-like and realistic it will be.

Try to involve all your senses by asking yourself what the relevant features are. Are there any particular colours in the background? What details do you see? What do you see in the foreground? Can you smell any special aroma or fragrance? What sounds do you hear? Are there any distinctive tastes or sensations associated with this place? Are there special friends or relatives there? Look at their faces, hear their voices. What are they wearing? What time of day or year is it? Enjoy creating this special image, savour the warmth and harmony and feel the peace and contentment you always find here. Let the atmosphere flow over you, soak it up like a sponge and feel all your worries and anxieties evaporating and drifting away. When you are mentally absorbed in visualising your special scene, your mental, emotional and physiological systems are all unified and co-ordinated. Your body responds with calmness, you experience a reduction in muscle tension, your breathing deepens, your heart rate slows and your feelings of relaxation deepen.

When you have cultivated your own special scene, make a habit of spending a few minutes visualising it after you have completed the diaphragmatic breathing and progressive muscle relaxation exercises. This will help to establish the scene in your mind and will ensure you have instant access to this special place any time you wish to switch off fearful thoughts. Now that you have found your special scene, don't be afraid to return to it whenever you feel the need.

Thought Control

The Power of Your Mind

The power of the mind cannot be underestimated. What the mind can conceive, the mind can achieve with a positive mental attitude. If you can control your thoughts you can control your emotions, and if you can control your emotions you can control your behaviour. One of the major reasons why some people develop a fear of flying while others do not involves the way comfortable air travellers control their thoughts, feelings and behaviour.

If you were asked at this moment to feel anxious, happy or sad, I would say that you would find it difficult to make an immediate response without first having some relevant thoughts concerning these emotions. Basically, happy thoughts produce happy feelings, sad thoughts produce sad feelings and anxious thoughts make you feel anxious. What you think will affect how you feel and how you feel will affect how you respond. It is therefore impossible to think negative or depressing thoughts and expect to feel fantastic. It is impossible to feel relaxed and anxious at the same time.

Can you imagine how you would feel at the prospect of taking a flight tomorrow? At this early stage you would probably still feel anxious, which is quite normal, but you can switch off this negative thought by entering your special place. An image or an idea can produce physical changes in the body. How many times have you felt your mouth watering when you thought of your favourite meal? It is the thought of the food which produces the saliva in your mouth. The major factor involving your fear of flying is your mind — your thoughts — which have been created by your previous flight experiences or by any of the causes mentioned earlier. Many are besieged by thoughts of air crashes, sudden emergencies, fear of the aircraft dropping hundreds of feet, possible engine malfunctions, turbulence or that there is insufficient air in the cabin.

The Role of Self-talk

Your negative thoughts are usually accompanied by negative self-talk, which is generally subtle and spontaneous. In fact, you are probably unaware of what you are saying to yourself and how it is influencing your mood and feelings. Your inner conversation is a very important factor in your response and attitude towards flying. Those who experience general anxiety or suffer from phobias inevitably make statements to themselves that start with 'what if'.

When you decide to avoid a situation, you have probably asked yourself one or several of these questions: What if I panic? What if I lose control? What if I become ill? What if there's turbulence? What if there's an emergency? An amazing question was asked recently: 'What if the manufacturer put the wheels on top of the wings?' This type of negative thinking and self-talk can be extremely distressing and makes the initial symptoms worse, which further strengthens your fear and keeps the negative circle spinning.

Any increase in negative thinking and inner conversation can turn safe events into stressful ones and consequenty increase anxiety symptoms' which can lead to avoidance of the situation. No one is born with a tendency towards fear; this type of thinking and self-talk which you have practised over a period of time has become entrenched in your mind. It is not easy to break the habit of irrational beliefs. However, with consistent practice and mental discipline you can learn to substitute positive, constructive thoughts and self-talk which will change your pattern of thoughts and feelings about flying.

Some anxious air travellers say that when they are on the ground, with no plans to travel by air, they know that their irrational self-talk is totally illogical. Yet when the prospect of taking a flight looms ahead, they firmly believe that their irrational self-talk is factual and true. It seems as though their irrational thoughts, self-statements and feelings when facing a flight supersede their rational appraisal when not taking a flight.

A pattern of negative irrational thinking leads to negative self-talk, which then produces feelings of intense anxiety followed by a strong desire to avoid the situation. When this happens, the fear is the winner and the individual becomes a victim of the fear. Avoidance of a frightening situation is very serious, because while you gain some relief or reward from not having to endure the feelings of anxiety, you are further fortifying and strengthening your fear. When this happens, you invariably find it more difficult at your next attempt.

A lot of people think that turbulence or the noise of the engines causes their fear, but in fact the fear is triggered from inside themselves. The fear is not in the turbulence or in the engines. For example, there are people who say that tunnels scare them rather than saying they are scared in a tunnel or crowds scare them rather than that they are scared in a crowd. In fact, nothing is done to you to activate your anxiety. It is important to understand that essentially it is your thoughts and self-talk regarding the event that establishes the basis of your opinions and response.

External events happen. You evaluate them. You mentally talk to yourself, you experience feelings as a result and you move on. You then proceed to behave according to your feelings. In order to conquer your fear of flying it is essential to deal with the mental aspect of your difficulty.

Irrational Thoughts

The word 'irrational' means useless, senseless, meaningless, mindless and pointless, any of which can describe the thoughts that pass through the mind of a fearful flier. Some travellers have described how they are tormented by irrational thoughts and self-talk prior to taking a flight. It is also true that negative or irrational thought patterns can be transmitted from one person to another. Often, as a pilot is giving a lecture on the technical aspects of flying, during which he states that the plane can glide, looks of disbelief on certain faces can be observed. These individuals glance at the others, seeking confirmation of their disbelief, and seem to be relieved if they get a nod of acknowledgment. Initially they find it hard to believe the facts that the pilot has stated and this is part of the irrational aspect of the fear. When they eventually accept the reality of the information regarding the technology and let go of their unfounded opinions, they then start to progress forward with a positive attitude towards flying.

It is therefore important to maintain control of the mental aspect of the problem and start believing and accepting the positive facts. It is now time to face reality and put perception where it belongs. A strategy for developing positive thought control starts with the following.

1. Accept that your fear of flying is irrational and pointless.
2. Accept that you cannot control weather conditions, the design of the aircraft or the aerodynamics involved in flying.
3. Recognise that your fear is out of all proportion to any real danger in the situation.
4. Believe that you can interpret the situation in a positive and realistic manner.
5. Believe that with practice you can learn to control your negative thoughts, self-talk and fear response and in turn reduce your fear considerably.

In order to take control of your negative thought patterns, you must first acknowledge that brooding over the distorted opinions you have about flying is not the solution to overcoming your problem. It is essential that you make a conscious decision to establish control over your thoughts rather than indulging them and allowing them to free-wheel out of control. Remember, nothing will change without your desire and determination. It is now advisable, coupled with the above, to pause for a few minutes and become acquainted with the following four steps to help you recognise and challenge your negative thought patterns.

1. Identify your thoughts and what you are saying to yourself.
2. Stop that train of thought.
3. Challenge your negative thoughts and substitute positive ones.
4. Relax, loosen up and breathe deeply.

Thought Challenging

The techniques for thought control are very simple and effective and require regular practice. Learning to think positively on a routine basis will become a habit and it will become easier to apply this control if negative thoughts intrude prior to taking a flight or when actually flying.

Thought control involves stopping the progression of the 'what if' thoughts and self-talk which occurs so quickly and subtly that it can continue undetected for some time. You need to be alert to the onset of such thoughts and determine to take control of them as soon as you become aware of them. When you realise that you are preoccupied with frightening thoughts, make every effort to interrupt the flow by engaging in a mental or physical activity and applying your new-found relaxation skills.

Your thoughts can be elusive and intangible. One of the most successful ways to deal with negative thoughts and irrational self-talk is to write down the thoughts and statements that triggered your anxiety. This will help you identify precisely what contributed to your distress and will assist your positive thinking. Spend 10 minutes at this exercise in the morning and 10 minutes in the afternoon. (Do not practise this exercise late in the evening or before going to bed.) You can lessen the hold of your irrational thoughts by keeping a record of them. Ask yourself the following questions before writing the answers down alongside them.

- Is this thought a problem right now?
- Is this thought constructive or destructive?
- What am I saying to myself to provoke this thought?
- Do I really want this thought?
- Do I genuinely want to continue this trend of thought?
- Are these thoughts self-defeating or helpful?
- Are these thoughts based on reality or fantasy?
- Why am I upsetting myself with these thoughts?
- What positive proof do I have that this negative thought will actually happen?

When you have completed the above exercise, challenge the negative thoughts you have written down and substitute positive, reassuring thoughts and logical statements to counteract your irrational perceptions. These should be written in the first person, present tense and avoid the use of negatives. A lead-in to the first question is: Yes, this negative thought is a major problem. Your positive thought should be: I refuse to let this be a problem right now. An explanation with further examples will be given later in this chapter.

Compile a list of thoughts and self-talk that is positive, believable and with which you feel comfortable. By keeping a personal record of these thoughts, over time it will help you see your progression towards a more positive frame of mind.

The following figures show the progression of negative versus positive perceptions and, in addition to examples, an exercise on how to compose rational positive thoughts and positive self-talk. There are two different pattern boxes with the same headings. One shows negative and the other shows positive patterns.

Negative Pattern

Event	Flying
Perception	Dangerous
Evaluation	May be turbulence
Response	Anxiety
Reaction	Fear or avoid

Now you have to ask yourself if this is positive or negative thinking. Is it constructive or destructive?

Positive Pattern

Event	Flying
Perception	Safest form of transport
Evaluation	Turbulance is uncomfortable
Response	I can cope
Reaction	I am in control

Example 1

Negative thought:	I'm terrified the plane will crash.
Negative self-talk:	With my luck it will be the one I'm on.
Question:	What positive proof do I have this will happen?
Positive thought:	Statistics prove flying is one of the safest forms of transport.

| Positive self-talk: | I am stronger than my fear. If I don't think frightening thoughts I won't be afraid. I can handle my anxiety by breathing deeply and relaxing. |

Example 2

Negative thought:	I dread hearing the aeroplane door close.
Negative self-talk:	What if I panic when the door closes? There isn't enough air, I'll suffocate.
Question:	Is this a problem right now?
Positive thought:	Obviously the door must be closed for everyone's safety.
Positive self-talk:	No one ever died as result of having a panic attack. I refuse to be afraid and let my fear dictate my behaviour. There is plenty of air in the plane. There is a change of air every few minutes in the cabin. I can practise my breathing exercises. I feel calm and composed about the door closing.

Example 3

Negative thought:	I dread turbulence. I hope we don't hit any.
Negative self-talk:	I'll freak out if we do.
Question:	Is this constructive or destructive thinking?
Positive thought:	I understand what turbulence is. It's uncomfortable, but not dangerous when my seatbelt is securely fastened. It's just choppy air and can't harm the aeroplane.
Positive self-talk:	It makes sense to cope. I can control these feelings by relaxing, taking a few deep breaths and thinking about something more pleasant. I am calm and in control. I'm doing fine.

As soon as you feel yourself sinking into negative thinking, interrupt the thought pattern and substitute a positive aspect of air travel. Instead of putting obstacles in your way by giving yourself reasons why you shouldn't fly, start telling yourself why you should. It is a good idea to prepare yourself by compiling a list of positive thoughts and self-talk about flying. Refresh your knowledge regarding turbulence, air safety and the technical aspects of flying. Try to concentrate on the personal advantages of air travel, such as the following.

- We can have family holidays in the sun.
- I can travel with my spouse/partner on business trips.
- I can visit friends/family living overseas.
- I can expand my business interests abroad.
- I can pursue career opportunities that involve air travel.
- I can travel by air if there's a family or business emergency.
- It gives me more independence.
- It's a personal challenge to cope with my fear and will increase my self-esteem.
- Flying means I have more time at my destination.
- It's the most convenient and safest form of transport. It's certainly safer than driving.
- Being able to travel by air whenever and wherever I wish will enhance my lifestyle.

You should understand that blocking unwelcome thoughts and negative conversation takes time and practice. Accept that the frightening thoughts will return and that you will have to cultivate the habit of interrupting them. The aim is to challenge your thoughts and substitute factual information. Always refocus your thoughts on either a thought blocker, a physical activity or occupy yourself in an absorbing task or pastime. You will find that, with constant practice, you will become more proficient at dealing with the thoughts and self-talk that undermine your ability to travel by air. These thoughts will decrease in frequency, will only last a few moments and will eventually cease to be a problem. If you follow the simple instructions and spend the appropriate time daily as specified, you will be able to control and suppress these thoughts very quickly.

Mental Activities

You are now familiar with the fact that frightening feelings usually follow negative, frightening thoughts. If you can control these thoughts, your air travel anxiety can be reduced considerably. Thought-stopping involves identifying the unwanted thought and clearing it out of your mind as soon as possible by substituting another thought, mental task or activity. This can be achieved by applying any of the following thought blockers or substitutions.

Thought Blockers

The word 'stop' means exactly what it says. Don't be afraid to say it aloud if possible if your surroundings allow. Imagine the voice of an authoritative person from your past or present ordering you to stop doing something. Challenge the thought, then firmly wipe it out of your mind and calmly focus on doing something else.

Count:	Try counting backwards in threes from 100.
Repeat:	Try to repeat the alphabet backwards, remember a poem or do multiplication tables.
Focus:	Focus on correctly repeating a tongue twister.
Review:	Review dates of friends, or family birthdays, anniversaries or replay a favourite movie in your mind.

What you are aiming to achieve is to stop the unwanted thought, so breathe deeply and give yourself another task to help you refocus your mind on another topic.

Thought Substitution
Many find thought substitution a pleasant distraction. Here are a few examples.

- Visualise your 'special scene'.
- Reflect on a cherished memory or happy ambition you want to achieve.
- Dream about how you would spend the Lottery jackpot.
- Reminisce about the most carefree moments and times of your life.
- Think of your favourite people.

Physical Activities
Thoughts can be interrupted by using the following 'startler method' or by getting involved in physical tasks.

- An effective startler method is to place a rubber band around your wrist and tweak it whenever you find yourself mulling over irrational thoughts.
- Splash cold water on your face or run cold water across your wrists.
- Simple tasks such as catching up on telephone calls, letter-writing or writing up your diary are gratifying distractions.
- You can also divert yourself from negative thinking by getting involved in a favourite hobby, doing crossword puzzles, jigsaw puzzles or listening to your favourite music.
- Physical activities such as mowing the lawn, walking, dancing or practising a sport of your choice are also good anxiety-reducing strategies.

What the mind can conceive, the mind can achieve with a positive mental attitude.

It may help to make copies of the following template and fill it in each time you practise challenging your thoughts. By working on this exercise you will be able to identify your thought pattern and self-talk more precisely, which will help towards disciplining yourself to reverse these thoughts and taking a more positive approach.

Negative thought:
Negative self-talk:
Challenging question:
Positive thought:
Positive self-talk:
Thought substitution:
Mental activity:
Physical activity:
Relaxation skills:

All of the above will encourage you to think positively.

Confront your Fear

The most successful way to overcome any fear or phobia is to confront it, as it will not disappear by ignoring it. The longer you avoid facing your fear of flying, the stronger and more deeply entrenched it will become. When you avoid taking a flight, you either feel an enormous sense of relief by removing the anxiety or a feeling of disappointment or failure. Unfortunately, such avoidance only strengthens your fear further and your next attempt to take a flight will invariably prove to be more difficult.

Now that you have cultivated anxiety management techniques, you are ready to confront the fear by using them in conjunction with desensitisation.

Sensitisation

Sensitisation occurs when you learn to associate anxiety with a specific event. Perhaps you felt frightened at the prospect of being trapped when you heard the aeroplane door closing, when flying through turbulence or when the noise of the engine changed. Whatever the reason, if you experienced intense anxiety as a result, you developed an association between those aspects of flying and the feelings of anxiety. As a consequence, the prospect of taking a flight or merely thinking about it can be enough to trigger such a response. You have developed a reluctance to experience these feelings again, so you have avoided flying when possible. You effectively became sensitised to the experience. When this happens you are in danger of becoming an aerophobic.

Desensitisation

The good news is that it is possible to learn how to weaken the association between anxiety and the relevant flight-related situations that cause it through the process of desensitisation. This consists of learning to break the association of anxiety you have learned to attach to flying and instead learning to associate feelings of control and relaxation. It is impossible to feel anxious and relaxed at the same time. At the present moment your feelings of anxiety regarding flying are stronger than your feelings of relaxation. In order to travel more comfortably by air, you need to readjust the balance by learning to weaken your anxiety and instead developing your ability to cope and feel more relaxed and at ease when taking a flight.

Successful desensitisation occurs when you can enter a situation that causes much anxiety while feeling relaxed or comparatively relaxed. The important thing is that you can handle it. When you feel relaxed you will no longer feel anxious. The prospect of facing a fear you have previously avoided whenever possible may seem quite daunting. Over the years your fear of flying has intensified to such a degree that it must seem impossible to confront and conquer it in its entirety. However, don't worry about this. The fact that you can now face the fear and make it more manageable is a tremendous step forward. You can manage your fear by breaking it down into segments and learning to face each segment systematically in manageable steps, starting with situations that cause you the least amount of anxiety and progressively working through aspects of fear that cause maximum levels of anxiety. Instead of facing your flying fears directly in real life, you first confront them in your mind and learn how to deal with them one step at a time. This is what imagery desensitisation will help you achieve.

Imagery Desensitisation
The seeds of your fear of flying are in your mind. The feelings of anxiety which result from your thoughts are sufficient to block your air travel plans. The bulk of your air travel anxiety is associated with frightening thoughts, images and fantasies about the experience. Imagery desensitisation, which many years of research has proven to be effective provided it is practised correctly, will lead to a considerable reduction in anxiety levels.

The first step in imagery desensitisation involves compiling a list of situations and events that cause you the most anxiety. The second step involves grading these situations from one to 12, starting with those that cause you the least anxiety up to those that cause you extreme anxiety. The aim of desensitisation is to learn to stay calm in a situation that usually causes you to feel anxious.

This list will permit you to systematically progress step by step through a series of anxiety-related situations, starting with those involving minor degrees of tension, gradually confronting and coping with those that cause increasing amounts of anxiety and eventually being able to successfully confront and deal with areas which evoke extreme anxiety.

The fear of flying hierarchy list will help you clarify the flight-related areas that cause fear and illustrates how to grade them accordingly.

Fear of Flying Hierarchy

Steps	Situations
1.	You are at home discussing plans regarding the possibility of taking a flight.
2.	The evening before your flight, you make preparations for the morning.
3.	After breakfast, you secure the house, place your luggage in the car and drive out to the airport.
4.	You park the car, take your luggage and walk across to the terminal building, where you locate the appropriate check-in desk for your flight.
5.	You check in, receive your boarding card, proceed through the security check and continue towards the boarding area.
6.	Your flight departure call is announced, you hand your boarding card to ground personnel and walk down the air bridge towards the aeroplane.
7.	You board the plane, find your seat and hear the aeroplane door being closed.
8.	You watch the cabin crew demonstrate the safety procedures. You hear the engine noises starting up and the plane taxies towards the runway.

⟶

9. You listen to the pilot's announcement. The engine noise pitch gets louder as the plane accelerates down the runway and lifts off into the air.

10. The aeroplane climbs to cruising altitude and the engine noise pitch changes. The 'Fasten seatbelt' sign has been switched off and the plane turns and flies smoothly in calm weather towards your destination.

11. The pilot announces that there is turbulence ahead and instructs everyone to fasten their seatbelt. It gets bumpy for a few minutes as the plane flies through rough air, then flies into calm air again.

12. The pilot announces that the plane has commenced its descent. The engine noise changes in pitch, the undercarriage is lowered and the plane descends closer and closer to the runway and lands.

As you can see from the above sample, each step involves increasing amounts of tension. This list can include up to 25 situations and need not be limited to 12. When you prepare your personal fear of flying hierarchy, you may wish to break down the steps into less intimidating ones, but make sure that each step is increasingly more difficult than the previous one.

It is now strongly recommended that you compile your own fear of flying hierarchy on the blank diagram provided below, as some of these items or situations may not be suitable for everyone. (Blank copies should be made of this and other tables for future use.)

FEAR OF FLYING HIERARCHY	
Steps	**Situations**
1.	
2.	
3.	
4.	
5.	
6.	
7.	
8.	
9.	
10.	
11.	
12.	

Imagery Desensitisation Practice

Before practising desensitisation it is recommended that you familiarise yourself thoroughly with each stage of the process, which is described as follows.

1. Start by working through the relaxation routine outlined earlier.

2. When you feel very calm and relaxed, visualise the first flight-related situation on your hierarchy, the one that causes the least amount of anxiety, as though you are mentally looking at it on a big video screen. Try not to project, stay with that situation and imagine it as vividly as possible. Include all the relevant sounds, aromas, activities, people's interactions, etc. that you associate with the scene. Spend between 30 and 60 seconds visualising the situation.

3. The moment you feel any tension, relax immediately. Apply all your relaxation techniques — release the tension by breathing from the diaphragm, relax any muscle tension, use positive self-talk. Affirm to yourself that you are calm and composed and that you can control the tension.

4. Stop visualising this scene and mentally return to your special scene. Absorb yourself in it and focus on regaining your earlier feelings of relaxation. Remain with your special scene until you are relaxed and calm again. This can take approximately one minute, depending on your level of anxiety.

5. If a situation causes severe anxiety, only spend five to 10 seconds visualising it and immediately return to your special scene, then go back to the situation causing the anxiety and gradually build up the amount of time you can spend there.

6. Replay the flight-related situation in your mind and use any tension it causes as a signal to apply all your relaxation skills again.

7. Again, after visualising the flight-related situation for approximately 30 seconds, return to your special scene and stay there for as long as it takes to become calm and relaxed again.

8. In this manner you systematically confront flight-related situations, apply your relaxation skills, then return to your special scene until the flight-related situation weakens. It can take from two to four mental visualisations to reduce the anxiety, depending on its intensity.

9. After the anxiety has been reduced to more manageable proportions, if any anxiety still remains, visualise how you ideally want to be. Mentally see yourself in the situation as you want to be, more than anything else in the world. See yourself behaving, responding and interacting in a completely calm manner, in control of any anxiety that now presents itself.

10. When a situation has reduced or lost its capacity to evoke anxiety, proceed to work on the next item on your hierarchy.

11. Remember to progress gradually to more difficult situations on your hierarchy. Reducing anxiety usually takes between two and four visualisations. It is very important to feel relatively calm with each situation before proceeding to work on the next one.

12. Always finish each visualisation by seeing your ideal image. Start each practice session by imaging your successful handling of the previous situation before working on the next one which involves an increase in anxiety.

To successfully accomplish imagery desensitisation, regular practice is important and it is recommended that you spend about 20 minutes each day working through your fear of flying hierarchy to achieve the results you desire. This in turn will help prepare you to cope with real-life exposure to the flight experience.

Real-life Desensitisation

When you have completely worked through imagery desensitisation, the next step involves exposure to the real-life situation. The prospect of facing your fear in reality may send shivers of apprehension down your spine and you need to gather all your courage to do this. While you may experience some initial discomfort, make a personal commitment to persevere and practise on a regular basis. Burying your head in the sand (the ostrich treatment) is not the answer. The only way to overcome this fear is to face it and deal with it. It is imperative that you confront what you have side-stepped or avoided for months or years to conquer your fear of flying.

'Pierce the fear and go beyond' is a wise Chinese expression that is applicable at this stage. When you successfully pierce your fear of flying, you will find there are many opportunities waiting for you beyond the fear which will enable you to live a more enriching and fulfilling life.

The method for practising real-life desensitisation is similar to that of imagery desensitisation. However, when you are progressing into real-life confrontation, you may wish to enlist the help of an understanding friend to accompany and encourage you to face the various situations which are an essential part of the real environment of the airport.

A sample pre-flight exercise list is given below and as with the imagery hierarchy we have just completed, it is advisable that you compile your own, relevant to your specific flight-related areas of anxiety. When working through this, do not proceed to a new

---

PRE-FLIGHT
REAL-LIFE DENSENSITISATION HIERARCHY

Steps   **Situations**

1. Drive to the airport or have a friend drive you.
2. Park in the car park, wait a few minutes until you are ready to proceed.
3. Walk into the terminal building.
4. Explore the departures terminal. Locate the ticket desk and check-in areas for various airlines and destinations.
5. Examine the flight information monitor displaying flight departure times and boarding gate numbers.
6. Continue towards the security check area. Watch passengers going through, showing their boarding cards to security officers.
7. Proceed to the aircraft viewing area and watch the planes landing and taking off.

---

step until you have adequately dealt with the previous one. If necessary, break down these stages into less intimidating ones and gradually extend your time in each area. The main objective is to stay in the situation or area for as long as possible, break down the threatening feelings and use the anxiety as a signal to apply all your relaxation skills. Then, when you feel sufficiently calm and composed, proceed at your own pace and in your own time to work on the next situation.

Below is your plan for your pre-flight checklist; include on this table as many stages as you feel are necessary.

PRE-FLIGHT REAL-LIFE HIERARCHY	
Steps	**Situations**
1.	_____
2.	_____
3.	_____
4.	_____
5.	_____
6.	_____
7.	_____

Refuse to place mental blocks to your progress as you go through these procedures. Encourage yourself onwards, reminding yourself that you can handle this, and use your positive self-talk to convince yourself that you can do it. It is vital to believe in yourself. If you don't, no one else will. Finally, make a point of giving yourself praise for having had the courage to confront your fear and to learn how to control it, rather than allowing it to control you.

Always remember that you are stronger than your fear.

CHAPTER ELEVEN

Security and Terrorism

THE MAGNITUDE AND AFTERMATH of the horrific atrocities that occurred in the US on 11 September 2001 will be printed forever on the minds of millions of people throughout the world. The nature of these disasters was unprecedented in the history of modern civilisation.

As a result, the threat of terrorism and skyjacking now looms large in the minds of many air travellers who previously had no fear of flying at all. They admit that while they are still unafraid of flying, they have developed an intense fear with regard to airline safety and their trust in aviation security has been severely shaken. They are, however, reassured that these tragedies were not the fault of the pilots or the planes and were exclusively acts of terrorism similar to those perpetrated in other parts of the world. On the other hand, those who already suffered a fear of flying have had their beliefs further compounded that air travel is a dangerous form of transport.

Resulting from the combined expertise and knowledge of various organisations, a variety of regulations and procedures have been designed and implemented to enhance aviation security and to shore up vulnerable areas not previously identified. In a matter of weeks after 9/11 a report was published in *Flight International* which described how various international bodies throughout the aerospace industry immediately began working together to strengthen and streamline airline security worldwide. The following is a brief summary of this report.

- The International Air Transport Association (IATA) set up a Global Aviation Security Action Group to provide a readily available source of expertise.
- The United States Department of Transportation and the American Federal Aviation Administration set up rapid response teams to deal with emergencies.
- The International Civil Aviation Organisation arranged a high-level ministerial meeting on aviation security.
- Europe (ACI–E) commenced working to examine current security procedures and additional methods of improving all aspects of safety.

This might sound complicated and official, but it should be emphasised how seriously governments worldwide considered these matters and sprung into action immediately. Since 11 September 2001 the US, Europe and Australia have spent billions in connection with security.

Passenger safety and security begins from the moment you arrive at the airport and continues as you proceed through the essential formalities at check-in, personal security screening, passport and immigration control. These security procedures continue while boarding the aircraft and throughout the flight.

Due to these regulations it takes longer to check in, so give yourself ample time to go through these procedures. Usually two hours is sufficient for a short-haul flight and three hours for a long-haul flight. Sometimes at check-in you are given a card to read which lists items that are prohibited and you are generally asked if you packed your own baggage.

At security screening you will be asked to open or remove your jacket, possibly remove your shoes and place all pocket items, such as coins, keys or glasses, in a special tray. Mobile phones, handbags and all carry-on bags must be personally screened and under no circumstances should you have any sharp items in your possession. All nail scissors, pen knives, nail files and sharp objects will be removed by security officials, and as this may cause you delay and possible stress, make sure you pack these items in your main luggage, which was checked in separately at the check-in desk.

Discreet passenger screening by officials in civilian clothes is always in operation at all airports, and if you have noticed anything which you consider unusual, be assured that this has already been noticed and reported upon. Passengers can be randomly checked at any stage prior to flight departure.

Any inappropriate behaviour or comments, such as 'I have a bomb in my bag', will be taken very seriously. It is known that passengers who made such comments, even in a joking manner, have been taken into custody and airlines enforce a strict policy of refusing to accept them on their flights again. CCTV cameras are now installed at all vantage points. At major airports in the US and Europe, all baggage is now scanned in the presence of the passenger before it is even dispatched to the luggage hold of the aircraft. Every avenue of air safety and security is being explored and strengthened, both on the ground and in the air.

It is advisable to give yourself a personal security check before arriving at the security barriers. Place all coins, mobile phones, wallets, purses, spectacles, sunglasses and pens in a suitable place in your carry-on luggage. By doing this you will more than likely be granted a smooth passage when walking through the body scanner, but don't be alarmed if it bleeps as it picks up all sensitive metal objects — even the buckle on your belt can set it off. If your bag happens to be segregated for a 'spot check' you will feel safe in the knowledge that everything it contains is quite safe and that the matter is only routine. Again, it should be emphasised that these checks are in place to protect us and should not concern us in the slightest.

On board, all visits to the cockpit have been prohibited and cockpit doors are locked throughout the flight. For many years the section between the cabin and the cockpit on certain airlines has been reinforced to sustain all attacks and in the future this policy will probably be adopted worldwide.

Following the horrific events of 9/11, the US government employed armed guards on all international and domestic flights. The term 'sky marshall' is now quite common and they are in the process of being employed internationally. These specially trained personnel will travel incognito in the various cabin sections throughout the aircraft. They will be armed with low-velocity automatic weapons equipped to fire special bullets, which can maim or kill but cannot puncture the skin of an aircraft. The US has insisted that certain international flights entering US airspace must carry an armed, civilian-clothed sky marshall at all times. This might seem extreme to some but every country will be responsible for selecting their own sky marshalls and this is for the greater protection and safety of all on board. In Ireland it is likely that sky marshalls will be drawn from the army ranger wing and from special Garda units.

In the event of confidential intelligence regarding security threats of any kind being brought to the attention of any airport authority, the matter is immediately investigated. As we have noticed from news media reports, some airlines prefer to cancel flights when there is the slightest suspicion of danger rather than jeopardise the safety of their passengers.

Since 30 September 2004, visitors to the US are fingerprinted and photographed to help check passengers' prints against a secure database of terrorist suspects and criminals. It is estimated that about 24 million foreign visitors will be fingerprinted and photographed every year. These conditions are a prerequisite set by the US for anyone wanting to enter their country. Irish travellers will be checked at immigration points already in operation at Shannon and Dublin airports by the US authorities, and under no circumstances is there any reason for alarm. It is just a further security precaution that increases our safety in the air.

It would be impossible to refer to all the security precautions presently being enforced throughout the world and while some are visible, the public is not privy to every aspect. For obvious reasons this would defeat the purpose and some must remain confidential or they would not be effective. These new security regulations are the strictest ever imposed in the history of aviation and are exclusively designed to make air travel the safest form of transportation available.

CHAPTER TWELVE

In-flight Health — Deep Vein Thrombosis

AN INCREASING NUMBER OF people are taking more long-haul flights than ever before in the history of commercial air travel, and health concerns, especially with regard to deep vein thrombosis (DVT), are gradually becoming a major cause of concern for many passengers. In general, in-flight health should always be foremost in your mind and the simple suggestions described in this chapter will ensure you enjoy a more comfortable flight.

According to medical experts, DVT itself is not dangerous. The knowledge that we have today leaves many unanswered questions concerning the link between DVT and air travel. Several medical studies of this connection have been planned and the World Health Organization is spending €12 million on research into this area.

When flying on long-haul flights passengers are seated in the same place, immobile and in cramped conditions for long periods of time. Limited opportunity to exercise can have certain effects on the body, which may include muscle tension, dehydration and swelling of feet and ankles. Muscle tension can develop in the back, shoulders and neck. Dehydration can cause dryness of the eyes, nose and throat and swelling of the feet and ankles can occur as a result of fluid accumulating in the feet, which is caused by the effect of gravity. Prolonged inactivity may also pose a risk factor in the formation of blood clots in the legs.

When blood is returning to the heart from the legs it has to flow through the veins against gravity. In normal circumstances, when we are active and moving around the muscles of the leg act like a pump which assists this process. As mentioned before, a possible problem may arise if you sit in the same place for too long. As a result, blood could collect in your lower limbs and in very rare instances a blood clot could form.

Now what can we do about all this and who may be at risk? First let us start by looking at those conditions or circumstances that might be considered as leading to a risk of DVT:

- personal history of blood clots
- genetic blood clotting problems
- pregnancy
- women taking oral contraceptives or hormone replacement therapy
- obesity
- cancer
- varicose veins
- heart disease.

Risk increases with age but it must be stressed that not all aged people will suffer from DVT.

The symptoms are as follows:

- swelling or pain in the calf or the thigh
- extreme swelling of ankles
- vague blue-red skin discolouration at the area of pain
- numbness or pins and needles in the legs, arms or chest
- fever or high temperature after flying.

As you can see, this is not a very long list and most of those at risk would have to take some special care anyway, even in normal circumstances. It must be emphasised that the rare possibility of developing DVT is not exclusive to flying on long-haul flights — the main issue is that of prolonged immobility. For instance, a person sitting at home for long periods of inactivity could be at risk or a person travelling a long distance by bus or car could also be at risk. It doesn't apply just to those sitting in an aircraft. The symptoms are also very straightforward and easily recognisable. If you suffer any of these symptoms after flying, contact a doctor immediately, advising that you have recently been on a long-haul flight.

Let us look on the positive side: how we can prevent these symptoms from developing. Some experts suggest taking aspirin, but it is strongly recommended that you seek advice from your own family doctor, who will prescribe the appropriate dosage and conditions for taking this medication.

Flight socks or compression hosiery are readily available in chemists, surgical supply stores and airport outlets and are designed to give additional support. The extra support assists the flow of blood in the veins, which your legs need for proper circulation. It is also advisable to consult your doctor regarding the suitability of flight socks.

In-flight exercises are very important and the following illustrate a safe method of stretching and moving certain muscles that can become tense following long periods of inactivity. They can help you relax and also assist the blood circulation. You should spend a few minutes practising these exercises every hour during the flight. It is also advisable to walk around the cabin occasionally when it is feasible and it is not a cause of disturbance to the cabin crew or other passengers. Do not undertake these exercises if they cause any pain or discomfort.

- Exercise the calves of your legs frequently by simulating walking while seated.
- Stretch your legs and make circles clockwise and anti-clockwise with your feet.
- Gently roll your neck backwards and forwards and from side to side.
- Draw your shoulders upwards, forward, backwards and down-ward.
- Perform some knee lifts and forward body flexes.
- Hold each position for approximately five seconds and repeat five times.
- Avoid crossing your legs while seated.
- At your destination take some mild exercise to boost your blood circulation.

Avoid excessive or heavy meals prior to flying, as it is more difficult for the body to digest large amounts of food when we are inactive. Preferably enjoy a light nourishing meal before taking a flight and beverages such as tea, coffee and alcohol should be taken in moderation. During the flight, drink lots of non-sparkling water and fruit juices to avoid dehydration and practise the above exercises every hour.

To ensure that you enjoy a more comfortable flight it is suggested that you read the section relating to personal comfort in Chapter 15 of this book. By following the simple instructions above, you will be assured that you have done everything possible to avoid the onset of deep vein thrombosis, but if you have any doubts whatsoever, contact a doctor immediately on arrival.

CHAPTER THIRTEEN

Nutrition and Fear of Flying

IN ADDITION TO DEALING with the mental, emotional and physical aspects of flight anxiety and before working on your personal flight plan, it is important to be aware of the influence certain foods and stimulants have on psychological stress.

In recent years the relationship between nutrition, certain foods and substances and stress has been well documented and there are many books and theories published on the subject. Thanks to all this research there is a greater awareness of the fact that some of the food and substances we find most appealing and tend to turn to for comfort in times of stress can actually increase anxiety levels further. On the other hand, a proper, well-balanced diet can mitigate stress and certain foods can help to either stimulate or calm.

The following section outlines information and advice on:

- the effects of stress-related stimulants, such as caffeine, nicotine and alcohol
- the role of diet in stress
- dietary guidelines for stress/anxiety management.

Stress-Related Stimulants

Caffeine

Most of us enjoy a cup of coffee early in the morning. It helps us wake up and feel more alert. However, caffeine results in short periods of alertness followed by a drop in energy. After the initial buzz wears off, many people try to recapture the earlier feelings by drinking more coffee.

Caffeine Effects

- Caffeine, which is also found in tea, chocolate, cocoa and cola drinks, drains your body of vitamin B, one of the important anti-stress vitamins. Caffeine is one of the major culprits responsible for producing a stress response.
- It is a stimulant that activates the same physiological arousal response that is triggered when you are under stress, which results in an increase in adrenalin release.
- An excessive amount of caffeine can keep you in a state of heightened tension and can lead to rapid heartbeat, an increase in blood pressure, feelings of irritability, anxiety and nervousness and can cause panic attacks.
- It can also cause headaches, increases uninary frequency and interferes with sleep, especially if taken late at night.

A classic example of the effects of excessive coffee occurred when a gentleman, who had successfully completed a fearless flying programme some time previously, described how he had coped very well on his flight from Shannon to Chicago and could not understand why, throughout his week's stay in the US, he was becoming increasingly agitated and nervous. It transpired that he had been drinking copious amounts of coffee since his arrival there, considerably stronger and in excess of his usual quota.

When he reduced his coffee intake, to his great relief his symptoms also decreased.

Advice on Caffeine

The American Medical Association advises that a daily limit of two cups of regular coffee, approximately 200 milligrams, is quite sufficient for the average person. However, for those who are prone to panic attacks or generalised anxiety, the recommended daily consumption is 100 milligrams, or one cup.

As part of your pre-flight preparation plan, it is in your best interests to take stock of the amount of caffeine you consume. It is advisable to gradually reduce or avoid caffeine one to two weeks prior to taking a flight and preferably substitute either weak or decaffeinated coffee, herbal teas or fruit juices. This will give your physical well-being a boost and eliminate additional and unnecessary stress reactions.

Nicotine

Many people believe that smoking a cigarette helps them unwind, especially when under pressure. Smoking does have this effect for an extremely limited timespan, but the reality is that nicotine is as powerful a stimulant as caffeine.

Cigarette smokers absorb nicotine into their blood. The chemicals in the smoke are absorbed through the fragile lining of the lungs and move swiftly into the bloodstream and onwards to every organ in the body. Smoking prevents an adequate supply of oxygen from being absorbed and increases the absorption of carbon monoxide, which impedes the blood's ability to transport its full quota of oxygen to the tissues.

Nutritionally, nicotine reduces the body's level of vitamin C, a very important stress-coping vitamin, which may hinder the body's ability to deal with stress.

Nicotine Effects

- Nicotine is an ingredient in tobacco which when absorbed into the bloodstream leads to an excessive production of adrenalin.
- The effects are similar to those of caffeine, including an increase in muscle tension, constriction of the arteries and, according to experts, they stress the entire body from the brain to the immune system.
- Research has shown that smokers are inclined to be more anxious than non-smokers, irrespective of their consumption of other stimulants such as coffee.
- It has also been noted that smokers do not sleep as well as non-smokers.

In Ireland approximately 6,000 people die each year from smoking-related illnesses. To help put this figure into perspective, it is almost 10 times more than the number of people killed in road accidents each year.

Advice on Nicotine

Quitting smoking can be a major ordeal, but according to many former smokers the rewards are numerous. Not only do they feel a lot more relaxed and healthier, but they sleep better, have a greater enjoyment of the taste of food and are less prone to panic attacks and general anxiety. Overall, the effects of nicotine and caffeine are neither helpful nor conducive to relieving stress. In this modern non-smoking world it is becoming more difficult to smoke anywhere you want and you only have to look around you to see this. You cannot smoke in supermarkets, cinemas, public transport, theatres, office buildings, public buildings, museums and in Ireland you can no longer smoke even in pubs and restaurants. It is not surprising that in recent years all major airlines have banned smoking on board their aeroplanes, so what is incorrectly seen as a form of stress release for some apprehensive air travellers is no longer an option when travelling by air.

Alcohol

Contrary to popular belief, alcohol is not the solution to resolving air travel anxiety. It is usually the advice given by well-meaning friends of fearful fliers, who encourage them to have a couple of stiff drinks before taking a flight. However, drinking for social reasons is fine and a small measure of alcohol can help you unwind and relax, whereas larger quantities can have the opposite effect. Unfortunately, excessive amounts of alcohol can in fact increase anxiety.

Taking alcohol in the vain hope of blocking out your fear of flying is clearly not the answer. Many former sufferers admitted they firmly believed that drinking more would eventually block out their fear and terror. When this wasn't happening they started getting more anxious and continued to drink more, hoping that the next one would do the trick. Indeed, they said that while they coped badly when sober, they found it almost impossible to cope after a few drinks, especially when they were not used to alcohol. Some could not understand why, no matter how much alcohol they consumed both before and throughout a flight, they were still terrified. On arrival at their destination, the full impact of the alcohol consumed kicked in, and many admitted they were so drunk and incapable that they had to be assisted off the plane. They inevitably found it took a day or two to recover. Then they had to face a repeat performance on their return flight.

An investigation into the relationship between alcohol use and air travel anxiety, using 100 subjects, resulted in some startling findings. They showed that almost 80 per cent found that alcohol was completely useless and ineffective, 17 per cent found it reasonably effective but they were still somewhat apprehensive and only 3 per cent said it actually reduced their anxiety. The results of other studies have also shown that alcohol is not effective in reducing severe or chronic anxiety.

Alcohol Effects

- Alcoholic drinks are high in calories and low in nutrients.
- Excess alcohol depletes B vitamins, alters blood sugar and raises blood pressure.
- Alcohol alters our perception of reality.
- In many ways it is a drug of denial and can camouflage both mental and physical processes.
- One of the most common effects of alcohol in normal circumstances is that of dehydration. The inclination for many is to continue to drink more alcohol to quench their thirst, rather than water or fruit juices.
- When flying, two measures of alcohol are the equivalent of three at ground level. This results from a decrease in oxygen levels caused by reduced cabin pressure, which can intensify the effects of alcohol.

According to the Committee on Alcoholism and Drug Dependence of the American Medical Association, the real psychological effects of alcohol are as follows:

'Ingestion of small quantities of alcohol usually reduces feelings of anxiety and worry and causes a mild but general reduction of inhibitions. If drinking is continued beyond the small quantity level, euphoria and exhilaration, dysfunctional reactions such as aggression, antagonism, depression and psychosis will appear, as well as disruption of speech and memory.'

Advice on Alcohol

Fearful fliers are advised *not* to drink alcohol before a flight in the vain hope that it will reduce their fear of flying. What people are hoping for is that the alcohol will suppress their fear, but as the survey clearly indicated, this only happened for 3 per cent of people. In other words, the feelings of fear are much stronger than the amount of alcohol consumed.

Having taken the initiative to learn how to confront and conquer their fear of flying, many remarked that one of the greatest feelings was being able to alight at their destination clear headed and relaxed instead of feeling woozy, frightened and sometimes embarrassed by their behaviour. They felt that being able to control their anxiety by natural anti-anxiety methods gave them a feeling of independence and control, plus an increase in their self-esteem.

Diet and Fear of Flying

Many fearful air travellers say they rarely have anything to eat before going on a flight. They claim they are either too busy, too anxious, too nauseous or have a knot of tension in their stomachs. Eating a meal would be the last thing on their minds. When travelling by air, your normal meal time is frequently disrupted due to pressure of time and other commitments. It is important to eat a meal before travelling, as time is taken up by driving to the airport, parking your car, checking in and so on. By the time you have actually boarded the aircraft, taken off and been served a meal, you may find that you have unwittingly, been fasting for a longer period of time than you would normally. It is important to be aware of a condition commonly called hypo-glycaemia, or low blood sugar level, which can even occur a few hours after eating a meal.

Hypoglycaemia

In order to function effectively your body and brain require glucose. This is a naturally occurring sugar which is the power your body needs for energy in order to sustain life. Much of this glucose is obtained from what we eat, namely carbohydrates, bread, pasta, potatoes, cereals, fruit and vegetables. The starches in these foods are slowly converted into glucose, which can take about 30 minutes. Carbohydrates contain tryptophan, which stimulates the production of a chemical called serotonin in the brain. Serotonin has a calming effect, eases tension and can improve concentration.

When under stress or feeling low, many people turn to comfort food such as sweets, favourite pastries or special cream-filled deserts. Evidence suggests that such foods stimulate the release of endorphins, which produce the 'feel good factor'. However, simple sugars found in refined white and brown sugar breaks down into glucose in as little as five minutes and can cause problems. They tend to overload the system with too much sugar too quickly. Sugar gives a quick boost of energy followed a short time later by a low-energy feeling due to the upset balance of blood sugar level, as the body is not equipped to process large amounts of sugar rapidly. Sugar may give a temporary 'high', but it also activates the pancreas to secrete insulin to process the sugar. In some people the pancreas over-reacts and secretes extra insulin, which causes their blood sugar to fall below normal, resulting in hypoglycaemia.

A rapid depletion of blood sugar can occur in response to sudden or chronic stress. It can also occur when people under stress don't digest or absorb their food as well as they do under normal circumstances. This can result in their reserves of vitamin B becoming exhausted.

When there is a decrease in your blood sugar level, adrenalin and cortisol are released from your adrenal glands. This results in an increase in your anxiety level and your liver releases its sugar reserves, which redresses the balance of your blood sugar level.

Symptoms of Hypoglycaemia
Some of the symptoms of hypoglycaemia are similar to those experienced during a panic or anxiety attack and are characterised by:

- anxiety
- irritability
- agitation
- palpitations
- dizziness
- trembling
- hunger
- thinking and concentration slow down.

Advice on Hypoglycaemia
It is relatively simple to overcome or avoid hypoglycaemia by making certain changes in your diet. This involves reducing or eliminating as much as possible simple sugars and processed or refined foods from your diet. Instead, substitute fresh fruit and 'complex' carbohydrates. It is recommended that you follow the guidelines on the stress/anxiety management diet in the next section, which will ensure that you avoid the unpleasant effects of low blood sugar and that you are better prepared to deal with stress.

Stress/Anxiety Management Diet
When you reflect on the influence of diet and the effects of certain stimulants, it is obvious that a healthy body copes better with the unavoidable stresses of life. A well-balanced diet is a

solid foundation for good health. In our modern, fast-paced society, many people do not give themselves enough time to relax and eat a proper, nutritious meal regularly. We seem to snatch at food and this is especially true when we are confronting stressful situations or experiences such as flying. Many fearful fliers have stated that they have actually lost weight in the days or weeks preceding a flight as a result of worrying, sleeplessness and not eating properly. On the other hand, many complain of putting on weight as a result of overeating or indulging in comfort eating.

At this point it is advisable to take stock of your usual diet pattern prior to taking a flight. It usually comes as a surprise to many fearful fliers that they have inadvertently contributed to their own stress and anxiety. Many admit they are prone to indulging in comfort sugar-rich food, while others say they find comfort by either drinking excessive amounts of caffeine or alcohol, smoking more than usual or just snacking. When you reflect on the effect all this is having on your body and stress levels, it is clear that this is not the ideal strategy to combat flight stress and anxiety.

In order to function effectively, brain cells need more blood sugar and oxygen than the other cells throughout the body. You need nutrients to exist and your body supplies these nutrients in sufficient quantity, but when you are suffering severe stress you need extra nutrients and an imbalance could occur. Therefore it is imperative to be able to swiftly re-establish crucial levels to enable you deal with stress efficiently. Good nutrition provides you with a solid basis for dealing with stress.

Advice on Diet

The old adage 'you are what you eat' is still true today and specific foods, whether they have a stimulating or calming influence, can affect your mood. Cast your mind back to that contented, satisfied feeling you enjoy after eating your favourite meal. In the weeks prior to taking a flight, it is in your best interests to focus on eating a healthy, balanced diet, which will help reduce stress. The following are general guidelines on food and stimulants that are best avoided, along with suggestions for a low-stress diet and recommended vitamin supplements to help you combat flight anxiety and stress.

Reduce or avoid:
- caffeine
- nicotine
- alcohol
- food and beverages that contain white sugar
- refined and processed foods.

You will manage your stress better by ensuring you focus on the following.

- Eating a healthy, well-balanced diet — this will ensure you get a good supply of all the different nutrients your body needs.
- Eat three meals a day, including breakfast — your body functions better if you refuel it frequently.
- Eat complex carbohydrates, which are considered to be calm foods, for example, wholemeal bread, bran, grains, pasta and jacket potatoes.
- Eat protein, that is, foods containing tryptamine, which activates the release of energy-promoting brain chemicals that can give you a lift when stress drains your energy. For a natural stimulant, it is recommended you eat small amounts of protein, for example, lean meat, dairy products, cheese, egg products, nuts and vegetables.
- Eat plenty of vegetables — when under stress, your body needs calcium, which has a calming effect on your nervous

system. Calcium is found in leafy vegetables and is a good source of fibre. It is also found in dairy products and eggs.

- Eat plenty of fruit, which provides natural sugar not found in fibre and vitamins.
- Drink at least a litre of water a day.

Multivitamins

As you can see, certain stimulants and foods:

- can influence your blood sugar level
- can influence how your body processes nutrients
- can deplete important supplies of anti-stress vitamins.

When dealing with an extra stress load, as in the weeks prior to taking a flight, in addition to focusing on a healthy, well-balanced, low-stress diet, it is also a good idea to start taking multivitamins and minerals which include extra quantities of the anti-stress vitamins B, A, E, C and calcium.

- *Vitamin B complex*: will ensure the proper performance of the nervous system. Natural sources are found in beans, poultry, dairy products, fish and wholegrain foods.
- *Vitamin C*: described as the 'stress vitamin', of which we need a consistent supply since we are unable to produce our own. Natural sources are found in fresh fruit, especially strawberries and kiwi fruit. Recent research has shown that one of the many functions of vitamin C is that it helps maintain the adrenal glands, whose correct operation is essential to your ability to deal with stress.
- *Calcium:* if you decide to take a calcium supplement, it is recommended that it be taken in conjunction with magnesium, as they balance each other and work together.

Advice on Vitamins

Always take vitamins with food to adequately digest and absorb them. However, before embarking on a course of multivitamins, it is advisable to check with your doctor what vitamins are most suitable for you. A word of caution: vitamins are not a substitute for eating a well-balanced meal.

CHAPTER FOURTEEN

Frequently Asked Questions

THE FOLLOWING IS A list of the 70 most frequently asked questions during the past 10 years of the Fearless Flying Programme.

1) *Can the wings fall off?*
No, this is an impossibility. The wings are not 'stuck' onto the sides of the plane but are a solid unit running right through the aircraft. The cabin is actually built either above or below the wings.

2) *Can the wings be put on back to front?*
No. This would be totally impossible.

3) *Can turbulence damage the wings?*
No. The wings are stressed and flexed to absorb turbulence, thus decreasing the effects of turbulence, within the cabin. Winglets are now added to the wing tips to further stabilise the aircraft.

4) *Can turbulence damage the plane?*
The simple answer is no. The aircraft is built to withstand turbulence up to 25 per cent beyond its design limits.

5) *What are flaps?*
Flaps are an extension of the wings and are used at take-off to increase the wing area and create greater lift. They are extended fully at landing to cause drag, thus slowing the plane down in flight.

6) *What are ailerons?*
Ailerons are the small moving parts that are attached to the wings and are used to steer and turn the aircraft in flight. This is the same steering mechanism that was invented by the Wright brothers.

7) *Why do the wheels retract?*
The wheels retract to decrease the drag force.

8) *Will the wheels always come down?*
Yes. There is a design feature built every aircraft so that in an emergency the wheels will 'fall down' automatically.

9) *Is the plane always trimmed?*
Yes. The weight and balance is calculated before take-off for every individual flight and the plane is continuously trimmed throughout the flight, particularly during turbulence.

10) *How does the pilot know the route to his destination?*
The pilot knows the route by aeronautical charts and airport-designed documents known as 'plates'. The aircraft follows land-based radio navigational beacons that are known as VORs (see

number 11) and NDBs. The DMEs (see number 13) measure the distance between these beacons.

11) *What are VORs?*
VOR stands for very high omnidirectional range. These beacons are usually located in the vicinity of airports.

12) *What are NDBs?*
NDB is short for non-directional beacon. These are used to guide the plane to the active runway.

13) *What are DMEs?*
DME is short for distance measuring equipment. It is used for measuring the distance between the aircraft and the VORs.

14) *Are there back-up radios on board the plane?*
Yes, there are various back-up and emergency radios and radar equipment on board.

15) *How many radar screens are there on board?*
There are two, one for each pilot.

16) *Are some pilots better than others?*
No. All pilots are of equal status. It is one of the few jobs in the world where knowledge does not affect promotion. Age and seniority are the only requirements for promotion. If a pilot fails any of his/her skill checks, they are grounded automatically.

17) *Can passengers walking around the cabin unbalance the plane in flight?*
No. An additional weight factor is built into the weights and balance of the aircraft to allow passengers to walk freely around

the plane. The plane is also continuously trimmed throughout the flight.

18) I have seen passengers taking lots of hand luggage on board. Can this affect the balance of the plane?
No. A similar weight factor far in excess of what a passenger can carry on board is also built into the weights and balance component of the aircraft.

19) Is the luggage weighed before it goes into the hold?
Yes, all baggage destined for the hold of the aircraft is weighed at check-in.

20) After take-off I feel that the plane is going to stall. Is this normal?
This is just an illusion as the power of the engines is reduced. Also, the aircraft could be starting a gentle banked turn. Einstein said that it is quite normal to feel this way in an unusual situation when the brain is not getting all the correct signals from the senses.

21) Can a plane fly on one engine?
Yes. A twin-engine aircraft can fly so perfectly on one engine that one would not notice the difference. Even a large four-engine aircraft has directional control with only one engine working.

22) If all engines failed could the plane still land safely?
In the very unlikely event of this ever happening, the plane will glide. Boeing says that a 747 'Jumbo' flying at 36,000 feet will glide for approximately 150 miles.

23) The plane can actually glide that far?
Yes, the aircraft will glide as it is trimmed and balanced. As a matter of fact, space shuttles glide back to Earth with no engine

assistance whatsoever, hence the reason it deploys rear parachute canopies on landing.

24) *Can a plane land automatically?*
This is a very complex question, but essentially the answer is yes. However, there must be the same 'software' on the aircraft as there is on the runway to facilitate such a procedure.

25) *What prevents the plane from ascending higher than a certain altitude?*
The air that is drawn into the engine is compressed and ignited to form the gas that drives the turbines, as explained in chapter 5. However, as the aircraft flies higher the air gets thinner and thinner, thus reducing the amount of oxygen contained therein. The engine simply runs slower and does not produce as much thrust so the aircraft cannot ascend higher. The engine only runs slower and will not stop.

26) *How does the pilot stop an engine?*
The modern jet aircraft is a very complex piece of machinery, but overall the most effective way of stopping an engine is simply to deprive it of fuel.

27) *What would happen if engines failed over water?*
The jet engine has so few moving parts that it is virtually impossible for anything other than fuel starvation to cause its failure. Notwithstanding this, the slightest glitch on any instrument would be enough to cause the pilot to divert to an alternate airport immediately. Transatlantic flights use Shannon, Iceland, the Azores, Labrador, Gander and Boston as alternatives and at any given point along the route the aircraft is only one and a half

hours' flying time from any of these airports. This is a similar approximate lapse time as a flight from Dublin to Paris.

28) *Can a plane run out of fuel?*
No, that is impossible as the pilot takes on board not only sufficient fuel for his flight, but also sufficient fuel to take the plane to an alternative airport in an emergency, plus 25 per cent more than what is required for the entire duration of the flight.

29) *Is fuel ever jettisoned?*
No, fuel is not jettisoned, but in an emergency situation a plane will circle to burn off excess fuel.

30) *What happens if there is a bird strike?*
Bird strikes usually occur only at airports. Rotating tungsten blades at the front of the engine prohibit any direct danger to the inner section of the engine. However, it is now mandatory that in the event of a bird strike all planes must return and land immediately for inspection.

31) *I worry about mid-air collisions.*
There is no reason to be anxious. All aircraft are closely monitored by air traffic control and are separated by radar.

32) *I have seen other aircraft in the skies when approaching big airports.*
Other aircraft may be seen when approaching a busy airport and these are 'stacked' 1,000 feet apart in a circular holding pattern. On instruction from air traffic control, all aircraft descend as one unit to allow others to join at the top and exit at the bottom of the cylinder, so there is no risk of collision.

FREQUENTLY ASKED QUESTIONS

33) *Is it possible to open the doors in flight?*
No. When the doors are closed they are suction sealed and the cabin is pressurised to an altitude of 6,000 feet, thus making it impossible to open the doors.

34) *Can the windows be broken in flight?*
No. The outer cabin window is over a centimetre thick and made up of three separate layers. They are not made of glass as we know it, but of a substance called acrylic. What you touch on the inside of the cabin is only a plastic superstructure and not the actual window.

35) *Is there enough air on board the aircraft?*
Yes, there is an ample supply of oxygen on board at all times and this is generated by the engines and constantly changed within the cabin. If there were an emergency, individual oxygen masks would drop automatically.

36) *What is the black box?*
It is an indestructible electronic device that records every movement of the aircraft. It contains information that is essential in an accident investigation so as to ensure that a similar incident might never occur again. It is usually situated in the tail of the aircraft but in fact could be located anywhere.

37) *How many runways are there at airports?*
This varies by the actual size of the airport. Runways are mainly constructed into the direction of the prevailing winds. If the winds are westerly, the runway heading may be 280 degrees and its reciprocal would be 100 degrees, so every airport has at least two runways.

181

38) How long is a runway?
Runways can vary in length depending on the size of the airport. For instance, London has two parallel runways which are used simultaneously for landing and takeoff. Runway 27R in London is 3,902 metres long and 27L is 3,658 metres long. Both are 45 metres wide. At Dublin, runway 28 is the active runway and it is 2,637 metres in length.

39) Is it dangerous when an aircraft overshoots a runway?
No, this is a well-practised standard procedure that pilots use for various reasons.

40) Why would an aircraft overshoot?
The reasons are numerous and varied, but the most obvious one would be weather conditions.

41) Where would the pilot go if he could not land at his destination airport?
He would fly to his alternative airport. When planning a flight, part of the flight plan requirement is that the pilot gives two other airports (see Chapter 6). One of these would have a different runway heading to that of his destination. For example, Shannon would always be given as an alternative for all aircraft flying into Dublin.

42) Are runways inspected regularly?
Runways are inspected every few minutes by airport authority personnel to ensure that they are clean and free from debris at all times. This is now an essential requirement following the Concorde incident at Charles de Gaulle Airport in Paris in July 2000.

43) What is the autopilot?
The autopilot is a built-in radio navigational aid that tracks the aircraft from radio beacon to radio beacon. It is essentially a

stabilising system, which keeps the plane trimmed and greatly assists the pilot in flight.

44) *Can the pilot take over from the computer?*

Yes, the pilot can override the computer if necessary. Even though the modern jetliner is a flying computer, the pilot is in absolute control of the aircraft at all times. In other words, the computer is only there to assist the pilot.

45) *Is it dangerous to fly through clouds?*

No, it is not dangerous to fly through clouds as all commercial flights are automatically filed under Instrument Flight Rules and all pilots are qualified with this rating. Apart from this, all east-bound flights fly at odd altitudes, e.g. 31,000, 35,000 or 37,000 feet, and all westbound flights fly at even altitudes, e.g. 30,000, 34,000 or 38,000 feet, so they are automatically separated. Laterally, airways are 10 nautical miles wide.

46) *Why do planes fly so high?*

Planes fly high for two reasons. Firstly, because it is safer and in the unlikely event of anything going wrong, it gives the pilots more time to correct the situation. Secondly, the air is less dense at higher altitudes so there is less resistance and therefore the plane flies faster and performance is more economical.

47) *Why does the aircraft accelerate so quickly down the runway?*

Runways generally do not exceed five kilometres, therefore the plane needs to accelerate to its take-off or rotation speed in order that low pressure can be created above the wing. (See Chapter 5).

48) When landing, planes seem to fly very slowly. Is this dangerous?

Planes can fly at various speeds and the speed maintained at all stages during the landing procedure is 30 per cent above the published stalling speed recommended in the manufacturer's handbook. Because of its size and closeness to the ground, the aircraft looks as if it is flying slower than it really is.

49) What would happen if a tyre punctured at landing?

There are multiple tyres on the wheels of all commercial jetliners so this would not present a problem.

50) If you don't need an engine to fly, why is it kept on during the flight?

As we know, it is the wings that supply the lift that enables a plane to fly but an engine is necessary for sustained flight. As previously stated, if the engines failed the plane would glide.

51) What would happen if an engine caught on fire?

The pilots are fully trained for such an emergency and every engine carries its own independent fire extinguishing equipment.

52) Are engines independent of one another?

Yes, engines are totally independent of one another and each has its own set of instruments within the cockpit.

53) Are pilots ever breathalysed?

Not automatically and there must be a suspicion of consumed alcohol before such an action could be authorised. It would be very foolhardy for pilots to think that they could get to the cockpit unnoticed after consuming alcohol. There are so many checks and interactions with personnel before take-off that a situation such as this is practically impossible.

54) *What is jet lag?*

One experiences jet lag when flying east or west across the meridians through various time zones. For instance, the 7.00 p.m. flight departing New York for Dublin only takes approximately six hours' flying time and arrives in Dublin at 6.00 a.m. the following morning Irish time. As there is a five-hour time difference our body still reacts as if it was only 1.00 a.m. in the morning, New York time. It takes approximately two hours per day to adjust back to normal, therefore it takes about three days to recover fully from a transatlantic flight.

55) *What is the official language when pilots are talking to foreign controllers?*

The official international language of the air is English and all pilots and all air traffic controllers (ATC) are completely fluent in English. For instance, an Italian pilot flying from Rome to Paris must speak English, as an international boundary has been crossed.

56) *How does ATC know when planes are due to land or depart?*

Flight plans are mandatory for all commercial flights and this information is listed accordingly and then forwarded to a central controlling unit, which notifies all concerned when a particular flight is taking off and landing. Alternative airports are also notified if they are listed in the flight plan.

57) *What is a slot time?*

A slot time is the departure time of an aircraft leaving an airport and this is 'booked' into the computer well in advance of the date of departure. There is an allowance of 15 minutes each way on all slot times, and when a slot is missed, the flight could be delayed until another slot becomes available. Slot times regulate the flow of aircraft in the skies.

58) Why do planes leaving airports at the same time not catch up on one another?

Very simply, the fastest one goes first. All cruising speeds are also recorded on flight plans so ATC is aware of this.

59) I panic when I hear 'We have a technical problem'.

There is no need to. This term is used to describe a multitude of reasons that would be too complicated to explain in a few words. A technical problem could refer to a blocked toilet or an unserviceable galley oven. Suffice to say, it definitely does not mean that an engine is falling off.

60) Why doesn't the pilot give more information?

This has always been a matter for discussion, as some passengers like information while others don't. In general, all essential announcements and information are well balanced and relayed to passengers as and when necessary.

61) Is a heavy landing dangerous?

Strange as this may seem, a heavy landing is regarded as a good landing. This type of landing is utilised in wet conditions or when operating in cross winds.

62) I worry that the plane will not stop after landing.

As soon as the plane has landed, the engines are placed into reverse thrust, which quickly slows the aircraft down. However, pilots are trained to land the aircraft on a certain part on the runway called the 'checkers', which allows plenty of runway ahead for the plane to stop normally by gentle application of the brakes.

63) *Why do the luggage compartments vibrate at take off?*
The luggage compartments, or 'hatboxes', as they are officially known, are only a superstructure, like pictures on a wall, and can vibrate freely. Don't be alarmed or concerned about this as they are not the skin of the aircraft.

64) *What is the skin of the aircraft?*
Depending on each particular aircraft, approximately seven interwoven pieces of aluminium foil make up the skin of an aircraft. This is not visible from inside the cabin.

65) *Where is the safest place to sit on board an aircraft?*
Everywhere is safe on board an aircraft. For additional comfort, business class offers larger seats and more space.

66) *Which is more dangerous, take-off or landing?*
The answer to this question is neither. Whether it is the take-off, the cruise or the landing, every phase of the flight is prepared and calculated well in advance as a controlled manoeuvre.

67) *Can stress affect a pilot's judgment?*
In order to measure this effect, a recent survey was voluntarily conducted on an airline captain. For three days he was fitted with a stress monitor which indicated that he was much more stressed while driving from his home to the airport than during the flight itself. His stress levels dropped considerably when he commenced his pre-flight checks prior to take-off. His stress levels increased again dramatically while he was driving home after his flight.

68) Are charter/low-cost airlines as safe as other major carriers?
Yes. What happens in the departure lounges, together with the
non-use of jet-ways, the free seating within the cabin and the lack
of free catering on board, are all cost-saving devices controlled by
the airline company. Under no circumstances do these cutbacks
reflect what takes place on the flight deck, which is totally
controlled by the specific country's aviation authority.

**69) Does every airline worldwide operate the same safety
standards?**
Yes, they do. Basically, the world is divided into two sections: the
CAA (Civil Aviation Authority) based at Gatwick, England and
the FAA (Federal Aviation Administration) based at Washington,
DC, US and any aircraft operating in these jurisdictions must
comply with their stringent regulations.

**70) Are cutbacks affecting the pilots and maintenance in
general?**
The engineers and pilots operate in an exclusive area that is
totally exempt from all cutbacks. Safety takes priority in all cases
and under no circumstance is it ever compromised.

CHAPTER FIFTEEN

Personal Flight Plan

NOW THAT YOU HAVE worked through the programme, the next step is to take the reality test by planning a short flight, preferably accompanied by an understanding friend or family member. Advance planning and preparation will help alleviate stress and anxiety and increase your sense of control of the situation. The following section presents general information and advice to help you through the pre-flight preparation stage and advice and tips for enjoying a comfortable and relaxed flight. Use the suggestions as applicable to your personal circumstances, whether you fly frequently or occasionally on short-or long-haul flights.

Personal Flight Plan

- Allow ample time to make flight reservations.
- Allow ample time to reserve accommodation at your destination.
- Ensure your passport is up to date.
- Check with the relevant embassy if you require a visa.

- Ensure you have some currency of the country you are travelling to.
- Ensure your cheque cards are valid.
- Travellers' cheques should be kept in a safe place.

Medical

- Check with the relevant embassy or family doctor if you need vaccinations, inoculations or specific medications such as anti-malaria medication.
- Have any injections required well in advance of your trip, in case of side effects.
- Check with your doctor if you are taking medication that may need adjustment while travelling abroad.
- Always carry your medicines with you on board the plane — do not pack your medication in your main luggage.

Personal Comfort

- Wear loose, comfortable clothes and roomy shoes. At 30,000 feet the gases in your body expand by about 30 per cent, causing your clothes and shoes to feel tighter than at sea level.
- Lemon-scented wipes are refreshing to use during the flight.
- A small, pocket-sized water demister to spray on the back of your neck and pulse areas will help keep you cool and calm.
- Glucose or mint sweets have a refreshing and cooling taste.
- Eye drops are soothing, especially on long-haul flights.
- Moisturising cream helps relieve dry skin caused by the dehydrated cabin atmosphere.
- A small inflatable pillow will help ease the strain on your neck.
- Ear plugs will help exclude loud engine noise at take-off.

Diversions

Keep boredom at bay by amusing yourself with pleasant diversions such as the following.

- Reading books or magazines.
- Doing crossword puzzles.
- Listening to favourite music or talking books on a Walkman.
- Take along games or pastimes such as Travel Scrabble, Trivial Pursuit, a deck of playing cards, Solitaire or Cribbage.
- Hand-to-eye co-ordinated puzzles or gadgets can keep you occupied for long periods of time.

Before Flying

- Try to have a good night's sleep the night before your flight.
- Have a healthy snack or meal before leaving for the airport.
- Give yourself plenty of time for your journey to the airport, as rushing increases anxiety.
- If time permits, practise the relaxation routine before leaving home.

Flight Check-in

- When checking in for your flight, explain to the airline personnel that you are a nervous air traveller and request a seat you feel will be comfortable, whether an aisle seat, near the galley, toilets or the over-wing area.

On Board the Plane

- Mention to the cabin crew that you are a nervous flier.
- Settle yourself well into your seat, placing a pillow in the small of your back. Place a pillow behind the back of your head if your neck feels tense.

- Relax your arms along the arm-rest of your seat, keep your wrists loose and floppy and focus on keeping your fingers separated. It is very difficult for your body to tense up if you are genuinely focused on keeping your fingers and hands loose and relaxed.
- Check your body for tension and relax tense muscles — shrug your shoulders, keep them down and make sure they are not tensed up under your ears. Gently rotate your neck from side to side. Stretch out your arms and legs. Use your positive self-talk to remind yourself that you can handle this, that you are calm and relaxed and practise your diaphragmatic breathing.

Take-off

- At take-off use ear plugs to block out engine noise.
- Resist the temptation to slip into the white-knuckle syndrome by grabbing the arm-rests or the seat-back in front of you. Remember, when you grab the arm-rests, you tense the muscles along your arms, upper back and chest, which will interfere with your breathing.
- Go with the flow of movements rather than bracing yourself against them and trying to correct them.
- Continue to loosen any tension, relax and affirm to yourself that you are stronger than the fear.

In-flight

- If you feel any tension throughout the flight, immediately apply your relaxation skills. Nip it in the bud; don't allow it to build up.
- From time to time do some simple stretching exercises.
- Raise your legs by placing them on your cabin bag or briefcase, as this will help your blood circulation.

- Don't stay in your seat for the duration of the flight, especially on long flights. Make an effort to walk around the cabin whenever it is convenient.
- Drink lots of water and fruit juice to keep the effects of dehydration at bay. This will also reduce headaches and tiredness.
- It is important to keep alcohol to a minimum.
- If you feel you are becoming agitated, ask the cabin crew to bring you a glass of iced water. Sip the water very slowly, then rub an ice cube across the pulse area of your wrist. This will slow down your pulse rate and give an instant calm, cool feeling.
- If the flight encounters rough air or turbulence, make every effort to relax and go with the flow of movements of the plane. Again, avoid gripping the arm-rests.
- Focus on the nature of turbulence and reassure yourself it is uncomfortable but not dangerous provided that your seatbelt is securely fastened.
- Make an effort to concentrate on one of the pastimes you brought with you, which will help lessen the fear.

Descent

- Change of pressure at landing can affect the ears. A popping sensation, earache or even temporary deafness is not uncommon. These can all be overcome by yawning, swallowing or moving your jaw. An inhaler such as one you would use to clear a stuffy head can also help.

Continue to go with the flow of aircraft movements. Remind yourself that the engine noise changes are safe sounds and part of the normal procedure for landing the plane safely.

Congratulations! You did it.

Enjoy your successful achievement.

You faced the challenge and surmounted it.

Your final instruction is to celebrate!

Conclusion

YOU NOW HAVE A greater understanding of the nature of fear, the factors that maintain it and, most important, the tools to deal with it. In addition to this, you also have information on the technology and personnel involved in ensuring you have a safe, comfortable flight. Accept that you cannot be in control of the flight. You must leave that to the experts. What you must aim to control is your fear.

This book and the self-management programme are based on the courses which I operate personally, both on a one-to-one basis and in small groups of five people. Clients who have participated in these courses have sent me countless letters and postcards from every corner of the world confirming that they have conquered their fear of flying. This has also been validated by follow-up surveys, which report a 96 per cent success rate. I am reminded of a quote in one such letter saying, 'I am no longer handcuffed to the island.'

As I finish writing, I see another beautiful monarch butterfly fluttering among the flowers in my garden and I think of the phases of development through which it had to pass in order to achieve its ability to fly — an apt comparison to the various stages through which fearful fliers are obliged to pass before they also attain their 'wings'.

Butterflies are free.

Limerick County Library

Bibliography

Anderson, H. E., 'The Psychology of Aviation' in *The Medical and Surgical Aspects of Flying*, London: Oxford Medical Publication 1919.

Aronson, M. L., 'Group program of overcoming the fear of flying' in L. R. Wolberg and M. L. Aronson (eds) *Group Therapy*, New York: Hawthorn 1974.

Benson, Herbert, *The Relaxation Response*, New York: Morrow 1975.

Bourne, E. J., *The Anxiety and Phobia Workbook*, Oakland, CA: New Harbinger 1990.

Davis, M., R. A. Eshelman and M. McKay, *The Relaxation and Stress Reduction Workbook*, Oakland, CA: New Harbinger 1988.

Handly, R. with P. Neff, *Anxiety and Panic Attacks: Their Cause and Cure*, New York and Canada: Ballantine Books 1993.

Jacobson, Edmund, *Progressive Relaxation*, Chicago: the University of Chicago Press, Midway reprint 1974.

Jeffers, S., *Feel the Fear and Do It Anyway*, New York: Fawcett Columbine 1987.

McCullough, C. J. and R. W. Mann, *Managing Your Anxiety*, the Berkeley Publishing Group 1994.

Selye, Hans, *The Stress of Life*, revised edition, New York: McGraw-Hill Book 1978.

Wolpe, Joseph, *The Practice of Behavior Therapy*, 3rd ed., New York: Pergamon Press 1982.

Yaffe, Maurice, *Taking the Fear Out of Flying*, Newton Abbot, Devon: David and Charles 1987.